OXFORD

geog.3

NEW edition

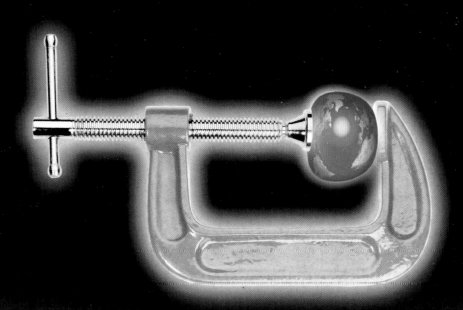

geography for key stage 3

<rosemarie gallagher> <richard parish>

OXFORD
UNIVERSITY PRESS

Great Clarendon Street, Oxford OX2 6DP

Oxford University Press is a department of the University of Oxford.
It furthers the University's objective of excellence in research,
scholarship, and education by publishing worldwide in

Oxford   New York

Auckland   Cape Town   Dar es Salaam   Hong Kong   Karachi
Kuala Lumpur   Madrid   Melbourne   Mexico City   Nairobi
New Delhi   Shanghai   Taipei   Toronto

With offices in

Argentina   Austria   Brazil   Chile   Czech Republic   France   Greece
Guatemala   Hungary   Italy   Japan   Poland   Portugal   Singapore
South Korea   Switzerland   Thailand   Turkey   Ukraine   Vietnam

Oxford is a registered trade mark of Oxford University Press
in the UK and in certain other countries

Oxford is a registered trade mark of Oxford University Press
in the UK and in certain other countries

© RoseMarie Gallagher, Richard Parish 2005

The moral rights of the author have been asserted

Database right Oxford University Press (maker)

First published 2002
Second Edition 2005

British Library Cataloguing in Publication Data

Data available

ISBN-13: 978-0-19-913451-9
ISBN-10: 0-19-913451-0

10 9 8 7 6 5 4 3 2

Printed in Singapore by KHL Printing Co Pte Ltd

Acknowledgements

The publisher and authors would like to thank the following for permission to use
photographs and other copyright material:

P4 Wolfgang Kaehler/Corbis Uk Ltd; p6 Nik Wheeler/Corbis UK Ltd.; P8 Guy Mansfield/Panos;
p10tl Corel/Oxford University Press; p10cl Corel/Oxford University Press; p10bl Corel/Oxford
University Press; p10tc Corel/Oxford University Press; p10bc ©LWA-Sharie Kennedy/Corbis UK
Ltd.; p10tr Corel/Oxford University Press; p10cr Corel/Oxford University Press; p10br
Corel/Oxford University Press; p10c Corel/Oxford University Press; p11 Corbis UK Ltd.; p12tl
Jorgen Schytte/Still Pictures; p12cl John Isaac/Still Pictures; p12bl Michael
MacIntyre/Hutchison Picture Library; p12tc Pat Bennett/Alamy; p12bc Penny Tweedie/Corbis
UK Ltd.; p12tr Ron Giling/Still Pictures; p12cr Michael MacIntyre/Hutchison Picture Library;
p12br Ron Gilling/Still Pictures; p13tl Jorgen Schytte/Still Pictures; p13tc Ron Giling/Still
Pictures; p13tr Popperfoto/Alamy; p14l Gary Cook/Alamy; p14tr Hutchison/Eye Ubiquitous;
p14br Pat Bennett/Alamy; p16 Jorgen Schytte/Still Pictures; p17 Jorgen Schytte/Still Pictures;
p19cl B. Apicella/Photofusion Picture Library; p19l E. Guigenan-Christian Aid/Still Pictures;
p19cr Ed Eckstein/Corbis UK Ltd.; p19r Harmut Schwarzbach/Still Pictures; p21 Anna
Tully/Panos Pictures; p24bl Nick Haslam/Hutchison Picture Library; p24br Corbis UK Ltd.; p24t
Ron Giling/Still Pictures; p25 Liba Taylor/Panos Pictures; p27 J.C. Tordai/Hutchison Library;
p28 Ron Giling/Still Pictures; p29 Gallo Images/Corbis UK Ltd.; p30tl Caroline Penn/Corbis
UK Ltd.; p30tr PA Photos/EPA/Empics; p30b Jorgen Schytte/Still Pictures; p31 Jorgen
Schytte/Still Pictures; p32 Reuters/Alamy; P34 Corbis Royalty Free; p37 Private
Collection/Bridgeman Art Library; p38t Panos Pictures; p38b Philip Wolmuth/Panos Pictures;
p40t Tony Waltham/Geophotos; p40b PA Photos/Empics; p41t Sherwood Energy Village Ltd;
p41b Sherwood Energy Village Ltd; p42tl Gideon Mendel/Corbis UK Ltd.; p42tc Zooid
Pictures; p42bc Ken Naylor/Capricorn MCS; p42tr CDC / James Gathanay/Science Photo
Library; p42br Allan Milligan/Scottish Viewpoint; p43 Pamela Grigg/The Scotsman
Publications Ltd; p42bl Photodisc/Oxford University Press;p44tl Dave G. Houser/Corbis UK
Ltd.; p44cl CharlesO'Rear/Corbis UK Ltd.; p44bl Ray Roberts/Rex Features; p44bc Owen
Franken/Corbis UK Ltd.; p44tr Larry Lee Photography/Corbis UK Ltd.; p44cr
GailMooney/Corbis UK Ltd.; p44br Karl Weatherly/Corbis UK Ltd.; p46l Soissons/Agence
Images /Alamy; p46r Franz-MarcFrei/Corbis UK Ltd.; p50l Art Kowalsky/Alamy; p50r Adam
Woolfitt/Corbis UK Ltd.; p54t Susan Anthony; p54c Susan Anthony; p54b Susan Anthony; p56
Yann Arthus-Bertrand/Corbis UK Ltd.; p57tl Hutchison Picture Library; p57cl Sarah
Murray/Hutchison Picture Library; p57tr Jacques Graf/Editing/Panos Pictures; p57cr Sarah
Murray/Hutchison Picture Library; p57b Pictor International/ImageState/Alamy; p58 Eric
Morency/EPAMarne / EPAFrance - Etablissements Publics de Marne-La-
Vallée; p59l Photothèque Epamarne/E.Morency, 1996/EPAMarne / EPAFrance -
Etablissements Publics d'Aménagement de Marne-La-Vallée; p59c Photothèque
Epamarne/Besse, 1988/EPAMarne / EPAFrance - Etablissements Publics d'Aménagement de
Marne-La-Vallée; p59r Photothèque Epamarne/E.Morency, 1998/EPAMarne / EPAFrance -
Etablissements Publics d'Aménagement de Marne-La-Vallée; p60l David Turnley/Corbis UK
Ltd.; p60r Drew Gardner/Rex Features; p62 Alamy Images p66tl Don Ryan/AP Photo; p66cl
George Hall/Corbis UK Ltd.; p66bl Daniel O'Leary/Panos Pictures; p66tc Getty Images; p66bc
Duomo/Corbis UK Ltd.; p66tr Getty Images; p66br foybles/Alamy; p66c Anat Givon/AP Photo;
p68 Corel/Oxford University Press; p69 Toby Adamson/Still Pictures; p70t Chris
Stowers/Panos Pictures; p70b Paul A. Souders/Corbis UK Ltd.; p71 Martin Sookias/Oxford
University Press; p72t The Photolibrary Wales/Alamy; p72c Emyr Rhys Williams; p72b David
Gibson/Photofusion Picture Library; p74tl Paul A. Souders/Corbis UK Ltd.; p74cl
Bettmann/Corbis UK Ltd.; p74bl Lito C. Uyan/Corbis UK Ltd.; p74tr Charles O'Rear/Corbis UK
Ltd.; p74cr Paul A. Souders/Corbis UK Ltd.; p74br Paul A. Souders/Corbis UK Ltd.; p75t
Donald Stampfli/AP Photo; p75b Corbis UK Ltd.; p76tl Anders Gunnartz/Panos Pictures;
p76cl Harmut Schwarzbach/Still Pictures; p76bl David Reed/Panos Pictures; p76tr Ron
Giling/Still Pictures; p76cr Mike Williams/Peak Pictures; p76br Catherine Karnow/Corbis UK
Ltd.; p77t Paul A. Souders/Corbis UK Ltd.; p77b David Turnley/Corbis UK Ltd.; P78
Reuters/Luis Galdamez/Corbis Uk Ltd; p80bl Kennan Ward/Corbis UK Ltd.; p80bl Jeremy
Horner/Corbis UK Ltd.; p80l Mark Henley/Panos Pictures; p80tc Stephanie Maze/Corbis UK
Ltd.; p80bc John Isaac/Still Pictures; p80cr Jeremy Horner/Hutchison Picture Library; p80t
Henryk T. Kaiser/Rex Features; p82l Martin Rogers/Corbis UK Ltd.; p82r Corbis UK Ltd.; p84t
Paul Harrison/Still Pictures; p84c & b Oxford University Press; p85l Enzo & Paolo
Ragazzini/Corbis UK Ltd.; p85r Gideon Mendel/Corbis UK Ltd.; p87 Andy
Butterton/PA/Empics ; P88 Getty Images; p90t Doug Houghton / LGPL/Alamy ; p90c David
Hoffman/David Hoffman Photo Library/Alamy ; p90b Doug Wilson/Corbis UK Ltd. ; p91t W.
Perry Conway/Corbis UK Ltd. ; p91br PLI/Science Photo Library; p93tl Thomas Raupach/Still
Pictures ; p93bl Getty Images ; p93tc Bob Krist/Corbis UK Ltd. ; p93bc Sean Holmes; Eye
Ubiquitous/Corbis UK Ltd. ; p93tr Getty Images ; p93br dpa Picture-Alliance GmbH ; p94 Bob
Edwards/Science Photo Library ; p96cl Stumpf/Sipa/Rex Features ; p96cr Natalie
Fobes/Corbis UK Ltd. ; p96t Rex Features ; p96c dpa Picture-Alliance GmbH ; p96b dpa
Picture-Alliance GmbH ; p97 Owen Franken/Corbis UK Ltd. ; p98t Peak Pictures; p98b Peter
James Miller/Science Photo Library: p100l Mike Williams/Peak Pictures; p100r Peak Pictures;
p102 Peak Pictures; p104l Peak Pictures; p104tr Ivan J Belcher/Worldwide Picture
Library/Alamy; p104br Peak Pictures; p105 Peak National Park Authority/Ray Manley/Peak
Pictures; p106 Roland Seitre/Still Pictures; p107 Bettmann/Corbis UK Ltd.; p108l Roland
Seitre/Still Pictures; p108tr Michael Nicholson/Corbis UK Ltd.; p108br Leonard de
Selva/Corbis UK Ltd.; p109 Galen Rowell/Corbis UK Ltd.; p110cl M. Sewell/Peter Arnold
Inc./Still Pictures; p110tr Roland Seitre/Still Pictures; p110cr Norbert Wu/Still Pictures; p110br
Godard Space Flight center Scientific Visualization Studio/NASA; p110c NASA; p111t Vincent
Bretagnolle/Still Pictures; p111c Fred Hoogervorst/Panos Pictures; p111b Chris
Sattleberger/Panos Pictures; p112 Mark Henley/Panos; p114 Alamy Royalty Free; p117 Image
Source/Oxford University Press; p118l Ace Stock Limited/Alamy; p118r Sealand Aerial
Photography; p120tl Paisajes Españoles; p120tr Paisajes Españoles; p120b David
Cumming/Eye Ubiquitous; p122 James Davis Worldwide; p125tl Peru Nature Rainforest
Expeditions; p125tr Peru Nature Rainforest Expeditions; p125c: Corel/Oxford University Press:
p125b Michael S. Yamashita/Corbis UK Ltd.

Illustrations are by Barking Dog; Matt Buckley; Stefan Chabluk; Richard Deverell; Karen
Donnelly; Roger Fereday; John Hallett; Richard Morris; David Mostyn; Mike Nesbitt; Colin
Salmon; Mike Saunders.

The Ordnance Survey map extracts on pp. 40, 103, 118, and 126 are reproduced with the
permission of the Controller of Her Majesty's Stationery Office © Crown Copyright.

The map extract on page 55 is reproduced with the permission of Michelin Editions du
Voyage. The population map on page 48, by Olivier Belbéoch, is reproduced with the
permission of Editions Magnard, Paris.

The publisher and authors would like to thank all the individuals and organizations who have
helped during research for this book. In particular, and in topic order:

Tamsin Maunder and other staff of WaterAid; Kate Kilpatrick, Oxfam; Michael Busby; The Coal
Authority; Carla Jamison, SEV Project Manager, Sherwood Energy Village; Susan Anthony;
EPAMARNE (the Development Agency for Marne-la-Vallée); Alex 'Walter' Middleton; Michael
Gallagher; the International Coffee Organization; Eric Sprokkereef and the International
Commission for the Hydrology of the Rhine basin (CHR); the staff of the Tourist Information
Centre, Castleton, the Peak District National Park; Andrew Ashe; Mick Nisbet of Penwith
District Council, Cornwall; Natty Bayo of the Spanish Embassy Education Office; Patricia
Barnett and Tourism Concern, London.

We would like to thank our excellent reviewers who have provided thoughtful and
constructive criticism at various stages: Phyl Gallagher, John Edwards, Anna King,
Katherine James, Roger Fetherston, Philip Amor, and Michael Gallagher.

We would also like to thank Janet Williamson for both general and specific contributions to
the geog.123 course.

Thanks also to Ann Hayes, Pauline Jones and Omar Farooque for their invaluable help and
support.

Information has been drawn from many sources. We would like to acknowledge in particular:
the Peak District National Park website, the British Antarctic Survey Antarctic schools pack,
and an article about jeans in the Guardian of 29th May 2001.

Every effort has been made to contact copyright holders of material reproduced in this book.
Any omissions will be rectified in subsequent printings if notice is given to the publisher.

Cover photo: Getty Images and Hemera.

Contents

The big picture

This very short chapter is about a key skill in geography: asking questions. These are the big ideas behind the chapter:

◆ We learn a lot about the world from photos and other images.

◆ By looking at a photo in an active way, and asking questions about it, we can discover a great deal.

◆ The development compass rose helps you think up questions.

Your goals for this chapter

By the end of this chapter you should be able to answer these questions:

◆ What is the development compass rose?

◆ What kinds of questions should I ask, for each point of the compass?

◆ What can I use the DCR for?

And then …

When you finish the chapter, come back to this page and see if you have met your goals!

Did you know?

◆ In some cultures, people think you steal their spirit when you photograph them.

◆ So it's polite to check first!

Did you know?

◆ Photography grew very popular in Britain in the 19th century.

◆ By 1865, London's Regent Street had 42 photography studios!

Did you know?

◆ The first ever photo, on paper, was produced by a British man, Mr William Henry Fox Talbot, in 1835.

Did you know?

◆ Digital cameras mean job losses for thousands of people, who depended on film for their living.

Your chapter starter

Look at the photo on page 4.

What's going on here?

Who are the people sitting down?

Why are the children dressed like this?

Do you think the children are enjoying themselves?

No, I will not say cheese.

The geography detective

In this unit you'll find out what the development compass rose is, and how to use it to help you think up questions.

Still nosy?

A good geographer has to be nosy. Just like a good detective!
Remember the kinds of questions you can ask …

Where is this place?

How is the place changing?

Why is it changing?

Who are these people?

Who is affected by the changes?

How do they feel about it?

IRAQ

And here are some of the answers, for this photo …

◆ This place is in the wetlands of southern Iraq.
◆ These people are Marsh Arabs, who live on floating islands of mud and reeds. They belong to one of the world's most ancient tribes.
◆ In the 1990s the wetlands were drained, by order of Saddam Hussein, to drive out the Marsh Arabs. The area began to turn into desert.
◆ Many Marsh Arabs fled to the cities, or to refugee camps.
◆ This story may have a happy ending. In 2004 a project was started to reflood the wetlands, and restore them to how they once were.

Stuck for questions?

A detective must ask *smart* questions, to find out what's going on.
So must you, in geography. But sometimes it is hard to think of them.
The development compass rose will help.

Did you know?
◆ Some say the wetlands of southern Iraq are the site of the Garden of Eden …
◆ … and also the birthplace of Abraham.

The development compass rose

The development compass rose (DCR) is just a prompt to help you find out more about people and their lives.

It's based on the compass (N for north …).

You can use it in lots of different ways. For example to help you think up questions about what you can actually *see* in a photo – like the questions shown here.

N for Natural

Ask about the natural environment – climate, living things, water, other natural resources. And how people interact with it and affect it (for example by farming and building). Like these:

◆ *How big is this island of reeds?*

◆ *Do they use this water for drinking?*

W for Who decides?

Ask about power: who's in charge, who makes the decisions, who gains, who loses. Like these:

◆ *Who is the most important person in the photo, and why?*

◆ *Who is the least important? Why?*

E for Economic

Questions about money, wealth, poverty, aid, buying and selling, earning a living. and where the profits go. Like these:

◆ *Are these people rich, or poor?*

◆ *Can they sell the milk from the cows?*

Or for asking deeper questions about what goes on in the hidden world *behind* the photo. (You'll try that later.)

You can even use the DCR just to help you write descriptions. Try it out. It's fun!

S for Social

Ask about the people's way of life, and culture, and traditions, and relationships. Like these:

◆ *Where have the two in the boat been?*

◆ *Why is the middle hut different?*

Your turn

1 a Make a *large* copy of this DCR. (Use a whole page.)

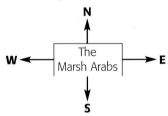

b Try to write in *two* simple questions for each point of your DCR, about what you can *see* in the photo. (If it's hard to decide where a question belongs, just put it where you think it works best.)

c For which DCR point did you find it easiest to think up questions? Why was that?

d For which did you find it most difficult? Why?

2 Here are two questions about life *behind* the photo.
N: What natural resources do the Marsh Arabs have, besides water and reeds?
W: Do the Marsh Arabs have a leader?
See if you can write one more question for each compass point, about the world of the Marsh Arabs behind the photo. (Put these in a different colour.)

3 Now turn to the photo on page 4.
  a Draw another large DCR for this, and write in as many questions as you can for each point.
  b Go through your questions, and underline the ones about the world *behind* the photo in a different colour.

4 Look at all the questions you wrote for 1–3.
  a Which do you think would be good enquiry questions? Underline these, and pick out the one you like best.
  b How would you do the research for this enquiry?

5 You can use a DCR to help you think up questions about nearly anything in geography – not just photos!

Volcano disaster in Chile!

You have to go to Chile and interview people, to find out what happened. Draw a DCR and use it to write down questions you will ask.

6 You can also use the DCR to help you describe places. Using the DCR as a prompt, write the text for a leaflet about *either* your school *or* your local area. (But don't use the terms *natural, social, economic, Who decides* in your final copy!)

The big picture

This chapter is about **development** – the process of change for the better. These are the big ideas behind the chapter:

- Development is about improving people's lives.
- It goes on all over the world, in every country, at every level. (It is even going on around you!)
- Every country is at a different stage of development.
- There is a big gap in development between the richest and poorest countries – so the world is a very unequal place.
- The interaction between rich and poor countries often benefits the rich countries at the expense of the poor ones.

Your goals for this chapter

By the end of this chapter you should be able to answer these questions:

- Development has many different aspects. Having enough money to live on is one. Which others can I list? (At least four.)
- Where is Ghana, and …
  - what are its main physical features, climate zones and ecosystems?
  - what natural resources does it have, and what are its main exports?
- What is life like in poor rural villages in Ghana?
- What are *development indicators*, and what six examples can I give?
- How developed is Ghana, compared to other countries?
- What do these terms mean, and which countries can I give as examples? (At least two different countries for each!)

  LEDC   *MEDC*   *Third World*   *rich north*   *poor south*

- What characteristics do LEDCs tend to have in common? (At least five.)
- For what kinds of reasons do countries fall behind in development? And what are some of Ghana's reasons?
- Why are many LEDCs in big debt – and how does it affect them?
- What goals have been set for 2015, to improve lives in LEDCs? (At least four.) And how could the money be raised to meet them?

And then …

When you finish the chapter, come back to this page and see if you have met your goals!

Did you know?
If the world were a village of 100 people …
- 14 would not have enough to eat
- 31 would have no electricity
- 17 would not have clean safe water to drink
- 29 would be aged under 15.

Did you know?
If the world were a village of 100 people …
- the richest person in the village would have more wealth than the poorest 57 combined.

Did you know?
If the world were a village of 100 people …
- 20 would be Chinese
- 16 would be Indian
- 1 would be from the British Isles.

Did you know?
If the world were a village of 100 people …
- at least 18 would have mobile phones!

Your chapter starter

Look at the photo on page 8.

Something new has arrived in this village in Ghana. What is it?

Why is everyone looking so happy?

Why didn't they have this thing before (like you do)?

Do you think there are many people who still don't have it?

That's shocking!

What is development?

In this unit you'll learn what 'development' means.

It is many different things

Development is about **improving people's lives**. So it's not just about getting richer, or buying more stuff. It has many different aspects.

10

Everybody's doing it

There are over 200 countries in the world. All are striving to develop. But some are further along than others. Some are developing very slowly – or even going backwards.

So there is now a huge gap in development between the most and least developed countries. That is one of the biggest problems facing our world.

Look back at page 10.

Your turn

1 Look back at page 10. The key aspects of development are outlined in red.
   a Write down this heading:
      Development – change for the better
   b Under your heading, list the other key aspects of development in what *you* think is their order of importance, with the most important one first. (For example would you put *the chance of a good education* first?)
   c Do you think everyone in the world would choose the same order as you? Explain your answer. (Compare lists with a partner, to check!)

2 Look at the drawing above.
   a What do you think it's trying to show?
   b What does it tell you about the UK?

3 Development costs money. For example it costs a lot to provide a clean water supply for everyone. From page 10, write down:
   a four other changes you think would cost a lot
   b two that may need people to change their attitudes
   c two that may need a government to pass new laws.

4 The photo below was taken in Iraq in 2003, after it was invaded by the USA and UK. War can halt the development of a country, or even reverse it. Explain why. You can give your answer as a spider map.

5 Which aspects of development do you think the UK needs to do more work on? Write a letter to the Prime Minister giving your list, and your reasons.

Now ... meet Ghana

This unit introduces you to Ghana – the African country we will explore in this chapter, to see how developed it is.

Welcome to Ghana

Welcome to Ghana, linked to the UK by history. Where you'll find ...

▲ ... a warm welcome for visitors ...

▲ ... tropical rainforest to explore ...

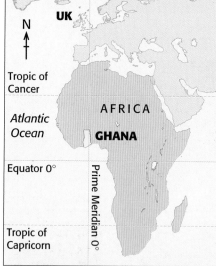

▲ ... some great wealth ...

▲ ... outdoor markets everywhere ...

▲ ... traditional ceremonies and rituals ...

▲ ... music, dancing, laughter ...

▲ ... a great sense of style ...

◀ ... gold and diamond mines ...

▲ ... hundreds of small rural villages ...   ▲ ... millions living in poverty ...   ▲ ... and a passion for football.

Ghana's physical geography

Look at the map on the right. You can see that over half of Ghana is quite low and flat.

The main river is the River Volta. In 1965 a dam was built on it to give hydroelectricity. A huge area behind the dam was drowned, forming Lake Volta, the world's largest artificial lake. It covers 4% of Ghana.

Now look at the shape of Ghana. It's quite neat and tidy ! That's because it was carved out of separate kingdoms by the British, by drawing lines on a map.
You'll find out more about its history later.

It's an LEDC

There are about 21 million people in Ghana.
Around 8 million of them live in great poverty.

Compared with many countries, Ghana is poor.
It is called a **less economically developed country** or **LEDC** for short. You will look at its development more closely later.

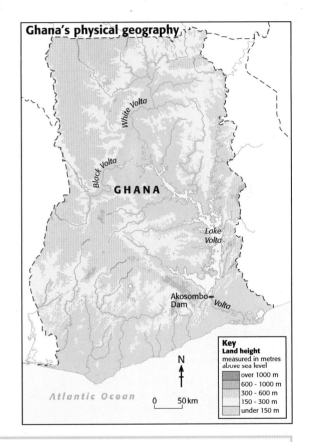

Ghana's physical geography

Key
Land height
measured in metres above sea level

- over 1000 m
- 600 - 1000 m
- 300 - 600 m
- 150 - 300 m
- under 150 m

Your turn

1 Where is Ghana? Use these words and terms in your answer: ocean, meridian, West Africa, tropic, equator.

2 Name the countries that border Ghana. (Page 129.)

3 Using the map above, write a paragraph about Ghana's features. (For example where is the highest land ? How high ? What about lakes ? Rivers ? Coast ?)

4 Using this table to help you, write a paragraph comparing Ghana and the UK. Give the *population density* for each country in your answer. (Glossary ?)

5 a Ghana is an *LEDC*. What do the letters stand for?

b What evidence can you see in the photos, that Ghana is an LEDC? (Give the photo numbers.)

Some statistics	Ghana	UK
Area (thousands of sq km)	240	245
Population (millions)	20	60
% in rural areas	55	10
Life expectancy (years)	58	77

A closer look at Ghana

Here you'll learn a little more about the geography and people of Ghana, before we go on to look at its development.

Ghana's climate and ecosystems

Ghana is in the tropics. That means it's hot! But like most countries it has different climate zones – which means different ecosystems too.

① hot and wet

- hot all year round
- about 2 m of rain a year

Tropical rainforest

- Ghana used to have a lot of rainforest. Only a quarter is left.
- It was cut down by loggers, by farmers clearing land to grow cocoa, and by people collecting firewood.

Ghana's climate zones

a hot dry NE wind called the *harmattan* blows December–March

Z•

②

Y•

Lake Volta

X• ①

③

prevailing wind

Atlantic Ocean

Did you know?
- About 400 000 tourists visited Ghana in 2000.
- They expect over a million tourists a year by 2010.

② hot and very dry

- it gets hotter than the rainforest
- one rainy season a year – and droughts are quite common
- the further north you go, the drier it is.

Savanna

- You'll see tall grass, and acacia and baobab trees.
- Desertification is a growing problem.

③ quite hot and dry

- quite hot all year
- two rainy seasons a year

Coastal savanna

- You'll see tall grass, thick-leaved shrubs, and baobab trees.

Ghana's natural resources

Ghana is quite rich in natural resources.

- The River Volta is important for hydroelectricity and fishing. The power station at the dam provides about two-thirds of Ghana's electricity.

- The forests are a source of timber. (So they're disappearing!)

- It has gold, diamonds, bauxite (aluminium ore), and manganese ore. They are found in the rainforest area, as the map on page 15 shows.

- It has some oil offshore (but not enough – it imports a lot more). It has far more natural gas offshore, which it began using in 2004.

- The hot wet climate in the south west is ideal for growing cocoa, for chocolate. So Ghana is the second largest cocoa producer in the world. (Its neighbour, Côte d'Ivoire, is first.)

- It has many protected areas in the rainforest and savanna, where you can see wildlife: elephants, buffalo, lions, hippos, chimps, monkeys, birds, butterflies and more. These are starting to attract tourists.

Ghana's people

Ghana has 60 different ethnic groups. They were brought together by the British, who carved the country from a mixture of kingdoms. (More about this later.)

As a result of Ghana's history, English is its official language. But there are four other main languages. In school, everything is taught through English.

Where do people live?

The map on the right shows Ghana's main towns and cities. 45% of the population live in towns and cities, and the rest in rural villages.

Many of these villages do not yet have electricity or a water supply, and many villagers live in great poverty.

What do people do for a living?

Ghana is an **agricultural economy**. 60% of its workers farm for a living. In the south west, as the map shows, people grow cocoa and oil palms. (Oil from oil palms is used for cooking, and to make soap and cosmetics.)

There is not much industry (manufacturing) in Ghana yet – but the government has big plans to change this. 15% of the workers are in industry.

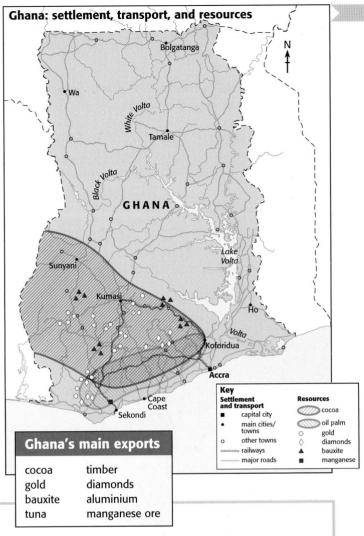

Ghana: settlement, transport, and resources

Ghana's main exports

cocoa	timber
gold	diamonds
bauxite	aluminium
tuna	manganese ore

Your turn

1 Using the maps on pages 12, 13, and 128–129 to help you, explain why:
   a Ghana is hotter than the UK
   b X on the map on page 14 gets more rain than Y
   c it's much hotter at Z than at Y, in January.

2 a What does *desertification* mean? (Glossary?)
   b Suggest reasons why it's happening in Ghana.
   c How is it likely to affect farmers? You could use a spider map or flowchart to answer

3 a Ghana has lost three-quarters of its rainforest. This process is called *de_____* (Glossary?)
   b How has it happened?
   c Who or what is likely to have suffered, as a result? (Use what you know already about rainforests!)

4 Study charts A–C on the right. Then write a report comparing Ghana and the UK, using these headings:
   Where people live
   What people do for a living
   The age structure of the population
   Use terms like *more than, less than, twice as many as* in your answer. And try to come up with explanations for the differences you find.

5 Ghana exports raw materials such as palm oil and cocoa. It has to import manufactured goods.
   a The government wants to set up lots more factories. Why do you think this is?
   b Come up with a list of factories it could set up – at least ten. (Think about its natural resources!)

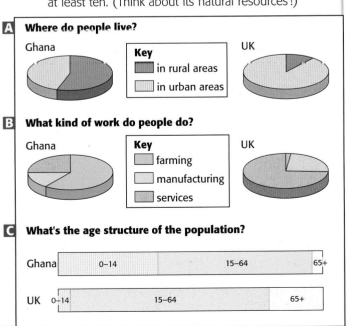

A Where do people live?

B What kind of work do people do?

C What's the age structure of the population?

Poverty in a Ghanaian village

Here you'll read about poverty in a rural village in northern Ghana.
(As in most LEDCs, poverty is worst in rural areas.)

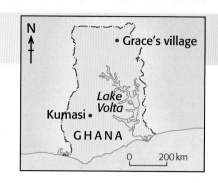

A day in the life of Grace

So you want to know what it's like to be poor?

I lie here on my straw mat, staring up into the darkness. My baby lies beside me, snuffling in her sleep. And over there on the mud floor my four other living children, all curled up together. Out in the yard, in their graves, the two dead ones. My firstborn died when she was three, and the youngest boy last year. How I cried when I buried them.

I lie here thinking about my problems. First, my husband. A good man. He works hard, and is always thinking of ways to make our lives better. Two months ago he went to Kumasi to find work. 'We will buy a goat with the money' he said, 'and send the eldest boy to primary school.' But I have had no message from him. He could be ill, or in trouble.

And the farm. The rains were poor last season. Out in our tiny field the millet is dry and stunted. Enough to feed us for two months, perhaps. What then? In the darkness I can feel my savings, tied in the corner of my cloth. Nineteen thousand cedis. If any of the children fall ill, that won't even be enough for medicine.

I could sell something – but what? You could count our possessions in seconds. Three enamel bowls. Two metal plates. The cooking pot. The water bucket. The kerosene lamp made from a bottle. The wooden pestle for pounding the millet. One machete. One hoe. Two small knives. A fork. A torch with no bulb. Two mats. And a few bundles of worn clothing.

But today is a new day. Soon I will rise and slip out to the clump of bushes behind the huts, which is the village toilet. Like the other women I go while it is still dark, for privacy. And at daybreak I will set off to get water. The river is nearly dry now, so the water will be very muddy and dangerous. It killed my children. But what can I do?

It takes me over an hour to get to the river, and longer to get back with my heavy bucket. I will give the children a little water to drink. I will breastfeed the baby. Then I will go to the farm to tend the millet and pick what's ready. And all day long I will hope that someone from the village will come running with a message from my husband.

While I am away my eldest daughter will pound millet. The eldest boy will go looking for firewood – every day a little further. Towards dusk we will eat our one meal for the day: millet porridge. At 6 it will get dark, as usual. I want to save the little kerosene that's left. So we will go to bed early, as usual – and, as usual, still hungry.

So, this is poverty. Coping with it takes all my energy. But we will survive, and I will find a way to create a better future for my children.

▲ Grace with two of her children.

Did you know?
- A child dies every 10 seconds, somewhere in the world, from a disease carried by dirty water.

Did you know?
- Ghana's currency is the cedi.
- 16 000 cedis equals about £1, in 2005.

▲ *Grace's village. All her friends are poor, like her. They all work very hard.*

Your turn

1 a List the items Grace has, for her kitchen.
  b Now list the things in your kitchen.

2

Time spent on tasks in Grace's household	
Task	*Minutes*
A preparing dinner (pounding and boiling millet, making a sauce)	200
B getting water (from the river)	170
C sweeping (the yard and hut)	45
D washing clothes (at the river)	200
E washing up (one meal a day)	20
F obtaining fuel (firewood)	120

  a Make a table like this for these tasks in *your* household. (Change what's in the brackets.)
  b Now draw a suitable graph to compare the times for these tasks in your household and Grace's.
  c Did you have any problems in drawing the graph for **b**? If yes, explain why.
  d For which task is the time difference greatest? Why?
  e For which is it least? Why?
  f In total, how much longer is spent on these six tasks in Grace's household than in yours? How might this affect Grace and her family?

3 Grace lives in great poverty. Draw a spider map to show what that means, for her. You could start like this.

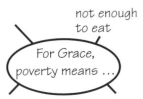

not enough to eat

For Grace, poverty means …

4 a Next, study the photo above, and note as many points as you can about life in Grace's village. For example note what the people are doing, and using. Which groups of people are missing? Don't forget to look in the background too. What are the houses like? Are there any electricity cables?
  b Now use your notes to write a couple of paragraphs about life in the village. Make them interesting!

5 You'd like to help the people of Grace's village. You can provide money and equipment to help them to:

  A install a village pump, giving clean safe water
  B read and write (so Grace can write to her husband)
  C fit solar cells (PV cells) to the hut roofs, so they can have electric lighting
  D build a latrine (a concrete toilet where the waste drains away into the ground)

  a Which do you think Grace would like first? Why? Write down all the benefits it would bring.
  b Arrange the four projects in order of priority, from Grace's point of view.
  c Who should have most say in deciding about the projects, you or the villagers? Give your reasons.

6 And now it's time to tell Grace about you.
  a Write a page about a day in your life, and the kinds of tasks you have to do, and what you worry about. (Imagine that someone who can read will read it out to Grace and her children for you.)
  b How do you think Grace and her children will feel about your life?

So – how developed is Ghana?

Here you'll see how development indicators can be used to compare Ghana with other countries.

Measuring development

On page 10 you saw that development has many different aspects.

You've seen that Ghana has a lot of poverty. But to get a clear picture of how *developed* it is, you need to ask questions like those on the right.

And then collect data to answer them!

Luckily the data is already collected every year for Ghana, and most other countries. It is published in tables of **development indicators**.

1 Does everyone get enough to eat there?

2 Do they have access to clean safe water?

3 Do they have access to medical help, if they fall ill?

4 How wealthy are the people, on average?

5 Can everyone over 15 read and write?

6 How long can people expect to live?

7 What are the chances of children dying before they reach five?

What is a development indicator?

A **development indicator** is just data that helps to indicate how developed a country is.

Look at question 6 above. **Life expectancy** is how long people can expect to live, on average. It is one example of a development indicator.

For people born in Ghana in 2002, the life expectancy was 58 years. For people born in the UK, it was 78. In other words, those in the UK are likely to live 20 years longer. (You'll try to explain why, later.)

Did you know?
On a scale called the human development index (page 19):
♦ Ghana ranks 131
♦ the UK ranks 12
out of 177 countries.

Did you know?
In every country women are likely to:
♦ live longer than men
♦ earn less than men.

Using wealth as a development indicator

One indicator that's used a lot is **gross domestic product** or **GDP**. It's the total value of the goods and services a country produces in a year. You can think of it as the wealth the country produces.

My share ....

... in theory.

Dream on!

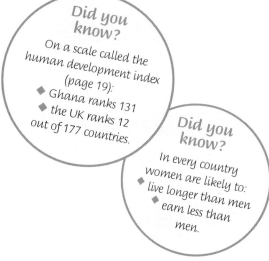

Little by little!

GDP per capita for Ghana	
Year	GDP per capita (US dollars PPP)
1960	$1043
1994	$1960
2000	$1964
2003	$2130

GDP is given in **US dollars (PPP)**. (**PPP** or *purchasing power parity* means the GDP is adjusted to allow for the fact that a dollar buys more in some countries than others.)

But some countries have far more people than others. Dividing GDP by the population gives **GDP per capita**. This gives you a better way to compare countries.

As a country develops, it produces more goods and services. So its GDP per capita rises. Look at this table. What does it tell you about development in Ghana?

But GDP per capita does not tell us whether people have safe water, for example, or enough doctors. That's why we need other indicators too.

Akosua, Ghana
Life expectancy: 58
Chances of –
  dying before age 5: 10%
  going to primary school: 59%
  a safe water supply: 73%
GDP per capita: $2130 (PPP)

Molly, UK
Life expectancy: 78
Chances of –
  dying before age 5: 0.7%
  going to primary school: 100%
  a safe water supply: 100%
GDP per capita: $26 150 (PPP)

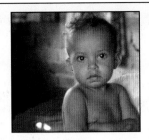

Maria Teresa, Brazil
Life expectancy: 68
Chances of –
  dying before age 5: 3.6 %
  going to primary school: 97%
  a safe water supply: 87%
GDP per capita: $7770 (PPP)

Prema, India
Life expectancy: 64
Chances of –
  dying before age 5: 9.3%
  going to primary school: 76%
  a safe water supply: 84%
GDP per capita: $2670 (PPP)

▲ *Comparing life in Ghana and other countries, using development indicators.*

Your turn

1 This table shows some development indicators.

The question	The matching development indicator	Its value for Ghana in 2003
	GDP per capita	$2130 (PPP)
	life expectancy	58 years
	adult literacy rate	74%
	under-five mortality rate	1 in 10 (or 10%)
	% with access to clean safe water	73%
	number of doctors per 100 000 people	9
	% undernourished	12%

  a Make a larger copy of the table. (Leave room to write quite a lot in the first column.)

  b Now write questions 1–7 from page 18 in the correct rows in the first column. (Glossary?)

2 Life expectancy is lower in Ghana than in the UK.

  a See if you can think up some reasons for this.

  b Do you think it will change as Ghana's GDP per capita rises? How? Why?

3 Next you'll compare Ghana with three other countries.

  a First make a table like this one.

	Score for ...			
	Ghana	UK	Brazil	India
Life expectancy	1	4		
Under-five mortality rate				2
Enrolment in primary school				
Access to safe water				
GDP per capita				
Total score				

  b Now look at the data for the four baby girls above. Using this data, give each country a score 1–4 for each indicator. (This has been started for you.) The country with the *best* result each time gets 4.

  c Find the total score for each country.

  d Using the totals to help you, list the four countries in order of development, the most developed first.

4 The **human development index** or **HDI** gives a quick way to compare countries. It combines data for GDP per capita, life expectancy, adult literacy, and enrolment in education, to give each country a score between 0 and 1. The higher the better!

Human development index (HDI), 2002

Australia	0.946	Kenya	0.488
Bangladesh	0.509	Mali	0.326
Brazil	0.775	Nigeria	0.466
China	0.745	Pakistan	0.497
France	0.932	Saudi Arabia	0.768
Germany	0.925	Spain	0.922
Ghana	0.568	Trinidad	0.801
India	0.595	UK	0.936
Japan	0.938	USA	0.939

  a Make a much larger copy of this vertical scale. Use a whole page. (Graph paper?)

  b Mark in each country from the table above, on your scale.

  c Now draw two horizontal lines, cutting the scale at 0.8 and 0.5, as started here.

  d Above 0.8 = high human development. From 0.5 to 0.8 = medium human development. Below 0.5 = low human development.

    i Shade each group of countries (high, medium and low HDI) on your scale. Use a different colour for each and add a key for your shading.

    ii To which group does Ghana belong?

    iii To which group does the UK belong?

HDI, 2002
1
0.5 ← Kenya
0

5 So – how developed is Ghana? And is it growing more developed, or less, or even going backwards? Give evidence to support your answers. (This little table may help.)

HDI for Ghana	
Year	HDI
1980	0.467
1990	0.511
2000	0.560

Mapping development around the world

Here you'll see how an indicator can be mapped to compare development around the world. And then you'll take a look at less developed countries.

An unequal world

The world is a very unequal place. You can show just how unequal it is by mapping a development indicator.

Look at the map below. It shows the **GDP per capita** (PPP) for different countries.

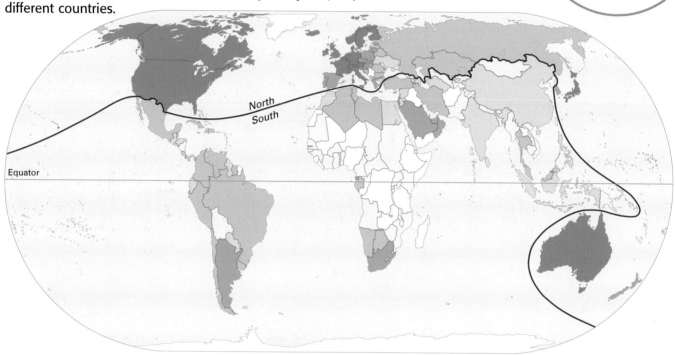

GDP per capita (PPP) around the world

As you can see, there is a big difference in GDP per capita around the world. Notice that many of the richest countries – with the highest GDP per capita – are clustered together. So are the poorest countries.

Many different labels are used for the richer and poorer groups of countries. See the main ones below.

Key
GDP per capita (US$ PPP)

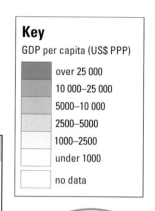

	over 25 000
	10 000–25 000
	5000–10 000
	2500–5000
	1000–2500
	under 1000
	no data

Rich North, poor South

Look at the red line on the map above. The richest countries in the world are above the line. The poorest are below it.

- So the richer countries are often referred to as the **rich North** (though some are south of the equator).
- The poorer countries are often referred to as the **poor South** (though many are in the northern hemisphere).

MEDC/LEDC

- The poorer countries are also called **less economically developed countries** or **LEDCs**. (You met this earlier.)
- The richer countries are called **MEDCs**. (What do you think that stands for?)

The Third World

- The poorer countries are often called the **Third World**.
- But some geographers don't like this term because they think it's patronising.

More about the LEDCs

Some LEDCs, like India, are very large. Some, like Trinidad, are very small.
Some, like Ghana, are in between. But all tend to have a lot in common.

... and surviving by farming

a high birth rate

... and women the poorest of all, with less education and less chance of paid work ...

... but working very hard without pay

... which makes it harder to set up industries

a high % of the population living in rural areas...

many people living in great poverty ...

poor infrastructure – roads, electricity supply, water supply and so on ...

LEDCs tend to have ...

not much industry, which means they can't make many goods ...

great inequality, with most people poor, but a small % very wealthy ...

... so have to buy them from other countries – or do without them

dependence on just a few primary goods (like cocoa or timber) for exports

high unemployment – many people can find no paid work to do

... but note that every country in the world has inequality

But LEDCs are striving to develop, and so they are always changing.
For example in India and China, industry is growing rapidly.

Your turn

1 Look at the map on page 20. In which range of GDP per capita (in US dollars PPP) is:
   a the UK? **b** Ghana? **c** Brazil? **d** Japan?
   The map on pages 128–129 will help.

2 Name:
   a five other countries in the same group as Ghana
   b five other countries in the same group as Brazil
   c five of the world's very richest countries
   for GDP per capita.

3 Assume for now that the MEDCs have a GDP per capita (PPP) of $10 000 or over.
   a What does *MEDC* stand for?
   b Name two MEDCs you haven't named already.

4 Write out each sentence. After it, write *True* or *False*.
   A Overall, Africa is the poorest continent.
   B Iceland is in the highest income group.
   C Mali is one of the world's poorest countries.
   D Everyone in Mali is really poor.
   E Overall, Libyans are better off than Egyptians.
   F The GDP per capita for Japan is $20 000 (PPP).

5 Do you think you'd get a similar pattern if you mapped life expectancy around the world? Explain your answer.

6 Find Cambodia on the map. Then, using the spider map above to help you, write 6 bullet points about development in Cambodia. Start like this:
   I think Cambodia is likely to have ...

7 So ... you've seen that many countries are poor.
   a Make a much larger copy of the DCR below.
   b On your copy, write down more questions you could ask, to find out why this is so. (Page 7 will help !)

Why are so many countries so poor?

Natural
◆ Is the climate no good for crops?

Who decides?
◆ Are their leaders no good?

Economic
◆ Have they nothing to sell to other countries?

Social
◆ Is it because they're too crowded?

How did the development gap grow?

In this unit you'll learn some reasons for the big gap in development around the world.

Three kinds of reasons

Here are the kinds of reasons why some countries lag far behind in development.

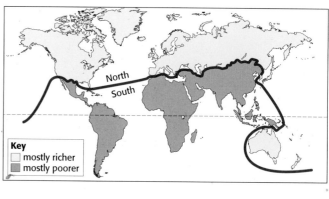

Key
☐ mostly richer
▨ mostly poorer

1 Historical reasons

Most of the world's poor countries were once taken over or **colonised** by European countries.

It started with friendly trading for things like gold, tobacco, timber, spices – and even slaves. But as time went by the Europeans grew greedier …

… and took over their trading partners by force. They took their raw materials, and sold them finished goods – and that made many Europeans very rich!

In time, the Europeans were forced out. But they left behind countries with little or no industry, or education, or skills – and often with a great deal of unrest.

Many of these colonised countries are still recovering.

2 Environmental reasons

These are to do with the natural environment. For example:

Some countries have very few natural resources they can trade to earn money for development. (But some deserts do have oil!)

In some countries the climate makes life difficult. For example rainfall may be unreliable, so it is hard to grow crops.

Some have the opposite problem – too much rain, and severe floods. Years of hard work just get washed away.

3 Socio-economic reasons

These are a combination of **social** and **economic** reasons. (Glossary?)

Many poor countries have wars going on, with much money and energy wasted in fighting.

Poor countries have few industries, so have to import most of the manufactured goods they need.

Most poor countries have borrowed a lot of money. Much of the money they make goes to pay back loans.

Most poor countries are striving hard to develop – but as you can see they face some enormous difficulties.

Your turn

1 a First, make a larger copy of this Venn diagram.
  b Now look at fact **A** below. Could it help to explain why a country is less developed? If *yes*, write the letter **A** in the correct place in your Venn diagram. (If you think it belongs to more than one loop, write it where they overlap.)
  c Repeat step **b** for each of the other facts **B – N**.

  A It is mostly stony desert.

  B It has plenty of copper to export but the price of copper has fallen sharply over the years.

  C It was a British colony for more than 50 years.

  D It is really mountainous and hard to reach.

  E A tribal war has been going on there for years.

  F The people who colonised it built no factories.

  G Millions of its people are suffering from AIDS.

  H There are few schools so people can't learn the skills the country needs.

  I It suffers serious flooding almost every year.

  J Bacteria and viruses that cause disease love its warm damp climate.

  K In the past, several million of its healthy adults were sold as slaves.

  L A small group of people owns most of its wealth.

  M Other countries refuse to trade with it, because of its politics.

  N It has to pay millions of dollars a year, for loans.

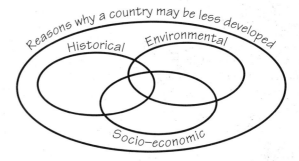

Reasons why a country may be less developed

Historical   Environmental

Socio-economic

2 Now write down ten reasons why a country (like the UK) may be *more* developed. Label them 1 – 10. Then show them on a Venn diagram like the one above.

3 What do you think this cartoon is about? Write a paragraph explaining its message.

So why is Ghana an LEDC?

Here you'll learn some of the reasons why Ghana is still poor – using ideas you met in the last unit.

Why is Ghana an LEDC?

You saw that Ghana has many natural resources, including gold and diamonds. It's the world's second largest producer of cocoa. Its people work hard. But millions of them still live in deep poverty. Why?

1 Some historical reasons

The first Europeans to arrive at the coast of Ghana were the Portuguese, in 1471. They found kingdoms of different tribes – and plenty of gold! They began to trade for it, in exchange for cloth, knives, beads, rum, and guns.

The news spread. Soon Dutch, Danish, German and British traders arrived too, in search of gold. The British called the land the **Gold Coast**.

But by 1650, the **slave trade** was more important than gold – because the Europeans needed workers for their sugar and tobacco plantations in the Caribbean, and North and South America. They bought over 100 000 people a year from the Gold Coast. The local tribes even started fighting each other, to capture people to sell! This went on for over 150 years.

Little by little, Britain took control of all the trade, and then the country. By 1901 the Gold Coast was a British colony. Its kingdoms and tribes were forced together, to make a single unit.

The British shipped gold, metal ores, diamonds, ivory, pepper, timber, corn and cocoa from the Gold Coast. They paid very little for these. They built railways to carry them to the coast. They built some roads and schools and hospitals too – but made the people pay for these through taxes.

In the end, the people had enough of their British rulers. They wanted freedom! At last, in 1957, the Gold Coast gained independence. It changed its name to Ghana. A free country – but with no factories, few services, and few skilled people to run it. (And that was only about 50 years ago.)

▲ Cocoa beans for chocolate. Ghana exports over 300 000 tonnes of cocoa beans a year.

Did you know?
- West African tribes had slavery long before the Europeans arrived.
- They sold criminals, and enemies they'd captured, to North African traders.

GHANA
• Elmina

▲ The fort at Elmina from which many slaves were shipped. It was owned in turn by the Portuguese, Dutch and British.

▲ These slaves were shipped to North America, and are being sold to plantation owners in an auction.

2 Some environmental reasons

60% of Ghana's workforce are farmers. So soil is a key resource for them. But soil is being ruined.

In the north, as you saw, parts of the savanna are turning into desert. This is caused by drought, chopping down trees, heavy grazing, and erosion of bare soil by wind and rain. It is called **desertification**.

In the south, three-quarters of the rainforest has been destroyed already – mostly by logging companies for timber, some by farmers for land to grow cocoa, and some for firewood. This is called **deforestation**. It gives people more land to farm – but the exposed soil is soon useless.

Ruined soil means fewer crops and animals. It means less food for farmers to feed their families, and to sell. So it means greater poverty.

3 Some socio-economic reasons

Ghana relies heavily on cocoa, to earn money. But the world price of cocoa goes up and down. So, some years, Ghana earns very little from it. (And meanwhile things Ghana imports, such as oil, get more expensive.)

Ghana has also borrowed a lot of money. So it has had to pay out lots of **interest** each year – which means less money for development. Other LEDCs have the same problem. There's more about this in the next unit.

Did you know?
Only a quarter of Ghana's tropical rainforest is left.

▲ *A farm in the savanna in northern Ghana, at risk of desertification.*

Your turn

1 You have to draw a time line for Ghana.
  a On a large sheet of paper draw a vertical time line from 1450 up to 2000. Make it 30 cm long if you can. (Use two pages?)
  b On your line mark in events from the text **and** the event box below. (Small neat writing!) Add a title.

2 Beside your time line shade the period in which:
  a West African slaves were bought by Europeans
  b the Gold Coast was partly or wholly a British colony

3 Now underline the events that you think:
  a *helped* Ghana to develop, in one colour
  b *held back* its development, in another colour
  c *did a mixture of both*, in a third colour.
4 Add a key for your colours and shading, for 2 and 3.
5 Choose *one* event you underlined for 3c above, and explain why you underlined it.
6 *'Since independence, Ghana's development has been completely under its own control.'*
  From the work you have just done, do you think this statement is true? Give your reasons.

(time line scale showing Year, 1500, 1450)

EVENTS

1878: a Ghanaian brings back cocoa plants from Fernado Po, an island off Africa

1528: chocolate drink from the Aztecs introduced to Europe, by Spanish explorers

1817: slavery abolished in Europe

1657: London's first drinking chocolate café opens

1928: a large harbour built at Takoradi

1502: first slave ship leaves West Africa

1965: the Akosombo dam completed, to provide Ghana with hydroelectricity

1980: economy almost collapses due to low cocoa price and other problems

1807: Britain starts campaign to stop the slave trade

1885: the first cocoa exported to Britain

1618: first British trading settlement set up on the Gold Coast

1874: Britain takes control of the south of the Gold Coast

1999: crisis in Asia and Russia causes world chocolate sales to fall

1993: Ghana earns $222 million from selling rainforest timber

1949: campaign for independence starts

1830: the world's first chocolate bars made in England by J S Fry and Sons

1898–1927: railways built by the British

1983: Ghana has to pay back loans of $1.5 billion to other countries

The problem of Third World debt

Here you'll see how development has been held back in many LEDCs (not just Ghana) by the big debts they have to pay off.

A burden of debt

As you've seen, many of the world's countries are very poor. They lag far behind in development. Millions of their people live in poverty, with no access to clean water, or toilets, or electricity, or doctors.

And one reason is this. These countries have to give millons of dollars every year to richer countries, to pay off debts !

Those payments affect the lives of hundreds of thousands of people in poorer countries. Many of them are young people like you.

How the debts arose

Poor countries want to develop fast – but that needs money, and they don't have much.

They do get some **aid** from richer countries. (They may have to make promises first !)

But aid is not enough. So they have to borrow money too. From **other governments** …

… or the **World Bank** (a joint bank set up by governments of over 180 countries) …

… or the **International Monetary Fund (IMF)**, a joint fund set up by governments for short term loans.

In the past they even got loans from **High Street banks**, for development projects.

Why the lenders were happy to lend

Much of the money was borrowed in the 1970s.

The lenders were happy because they had plenty of money to lend – and they would collect interest (a fee for lending) each year.

They did not think too much about what the money would be used for, or whether the poor countries could afford to pay the interest.

How interest adds up: an example
Loan: $1000 million for 40 years
Interest: 5% of the loan per year = $50 million per year.
Total interest over 40 years: **2000 million dollars !**

The result

If you borrow a lot of money, and don't earn enough, it means trouble!

Soon the poor countries ran into problems. They found they had to borrow more and more to survive.

And now a lot of the money they earn each year is used just to pay off debts. Which means ...

... less for schools, or hospitals, or a water supply, or the other things their people need badly.

Tackling the problem

It is clear that many poor countries will never be able to escape poverty, because of their debts.

So people in richer countries are putting pressure on their governments to cancel *all* old Third World debts. There is also pressure on the World Bank and IMF.

The good news is that Ghana and some other **heavily indebted** countries have already had some debts cancelled. In return they have promised to use the money to help their poorest people.

The UK has led the way in cancelling debt, and is asking other countries to follow.

▲ *The pressure is on ...*

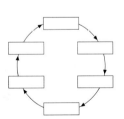

Your turn

1 a When you take out a loan you have to pay *interest*. What does that mean?

 b Ghana is *heavily indebted* What does that mean?

2 a Draw a circular flowchart with 6 boxes. (Like the one on the right, but much larger.)

 b Write the items below in the boxes, *in the correct order*, to show how a poor country gets further into debt. Give your flowchart a suitable title.

So it borrows more money.

So it does not earn as much as it had hoped.

The next year the country sells crops and minerals to other countries, as usual.

But it still has to pay the interest on its loans ...

But the prices for these have dropped again.

... which then leaves it short of money to pay for imports, and for development projects.

Did you know?
- The world's poor countries owe about $460 billion in total.
- Americans alone spend about $570 billion a year on gambling.

3 When poor countries borrow money, they may end up paying several times that amount back. See if you can explain why. (Look at the calculation at the bottom of page 26.)

4 Some of Ghana's debts have been cancelled. But it still has to pay over $100 million a year for debt. How might it help Grace if of Ghana's debts were cancelled? Give your answer in any form you wish. For example as a flowchart, or strip cartoon, or as a speech from Grace, or a rap.

A big dam ... to help Ghana?

In this unit you'll see how a big project, to help Ghana develop, did not turn out quite as planned!

The story behind the dam

When Ghana got its independence in 1957 it was in a hurry to develop. It wanted factories, schools, hospitals, roads, new homes.
All this needs energy. And Ghana had the answer: the River Volta!
A dam could be built on it to give **hydroelectricity**.

Dams cost a fortune. Ghana had no money. So it got loans from the World Bank and the UK, and a large loan from the USA. As part of this deal, an American company called Valco got the right to produce aluminium in Ghana, using electricity from the dam:

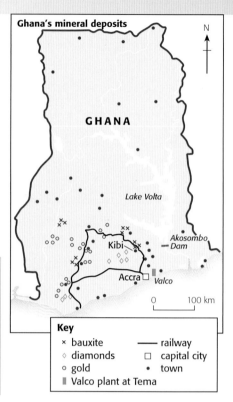

Ghana's mineral deposits

Key
× bauxite — railway
◇ diamonds □ capital city
○ gold • town
▮ Valco plant at Tema

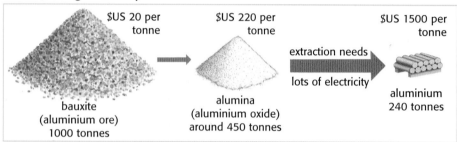

$US 20 per tonne — bauxite (aluminium ore) 1000 tonnes

$US 220 per tonne — alumina (aluminium oxide) around 450 tonnes

extraction needs lots of electricity

$US 1500 per tonne — aluminium 240 tonnes

Ghana was happy because it has a lot of bauxite. It promised Valco cheap electricity for 50 years. This is what Ghana hoped would happen:

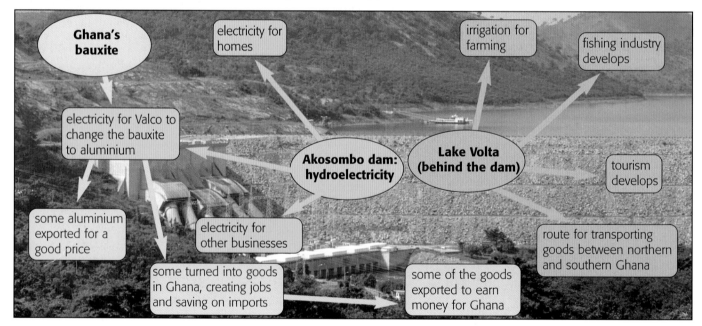

Ghana's bauxite

electricity for homes

irrigation for farming

fishing industry develops

electricity for Valco to change the bauxite to aluminium

Akosombo dam: hydroelectricity

Lake Volta (behind the dam)

tourism develops

some aluminium exported for a good price

electricity for other businesses

some turned into goods in Ghana, creating jobs and saving on imports

some of the goods exported to earn money for Ghana

route for transporting goods between northern and southern Ghana

The project gets going

Over 80 000 people were moved from their farms and villages to make way for the Akosombo dam. It created a giant lake, drowning 4% of Ghana. (Look at the map above.) It was completed in 1965.

Meanwhile Valco built an aluminium smelter (for extracting aluminium) at the port of Tema. It said it would import alumina from its mines in Jamaica until an alumina plant and railway had been built in Ghana, for using Ghana's bauxite.

How things turned out

The dam has helped Ghana in many ways. But things did not turn out quite as planned. By the year 2000, 35 years after the dam was finished:

◆ Valco was still importing alumina from Jamaica – and using none of Ghana's bauxite.

◆ It was paying much less for electricity than the local companies did. (And at times it used nearly half the electricity from the dam.)

◆ It did not have to pay a tax on the alumina it imported, or the aluminium it exported.

◆ Frequent droughts were causing the water level in Lake Volta to fall – which meant less electricity. So the government had to force Valco to use less, to allow enough for other users.

◆ Ghana had to export its bauxite. (Exporting aluminium would earn it a lot more, as the diagram on page 28 shows.)

◆ Lake Volta was not being used much for irrigation, or transport, or tourism (but it did get used for fishing).

◆ And most rural villages in Ghana still do not have electricity ! They depend on firewood for cooking.

The new challenge

Now Ghana faces a new challenge. In 2003 it said Valco must pay more for electricity. So Valco said it could no longer make a profit in Ghana. It wanted to sell its smelter to the government, and leave.

Now Ghana has the chance to use its own bauxite. But first it will need a plant to turn it into alumina, and a railway to carry the alumina to Tema. Experts say that will cost at least 1 billion dollars, which Ghana will have to borrow. Can Ghana make it work – or will it be money down the drain ?

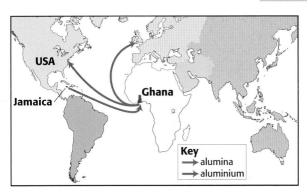

▲ Valco's aluminium routes.

▲ A traditional wooden boat called a pirogue, on Lake Volta.

Did you know?
◆ Ghana aims to electrify all its villages by 2020. (Look back at page 8.)

Your turn

1 What is *hydroelectricity*? What are its advantages ?

2 The diagram on page 28 shows what Ghana hoped for, from the dam. Draw a diagram to show what did in fact happen. (You could copy that one and cross bits out if you like, and add notes in a different colour.)

3 Page 28 shows the steps in making aluminium.
  a Suggest reasons why Valco:
    i did not produce the aluminium in Jamaica
    ii changed the bauxite to alumina in Jamaica
    iii did not ship the alumina to the USA.
  b To which country do you think Valco's profts went ?

4 a In which ways did:
    i Valco benefit Ghana ? ii Ghana benefit Valco ?
  b Which of the two do you think got a better deal?

5 'The Akosombo dam is a great example of sustainable development.' Do you agree ? Explain. (Glossary ?)

6 The Ghanaian government wants your advice. It has these options:
  A Ask Valco to stay, with cheap electricity as before.
  B Let Valco go, keep exporting bauxite, and use the electricity from the dam for Ghana's villages.
  C Buy the smelter and convert bauxite to aluminium for export. Then bring electricity to the villages later.

  a Write a list of pros and cons for each option.
  b Choose the option you think seems best – or come up with another.
  c Write a report for the government about your chosen option, and explain why you think it's the best one. Include a list of points the government should think about, before it finally makes up its mind.
    (For example how much it might need to borrow, or the problem of future droughts, or whether there's another way to electrify Ghana's villages.)

Small is beautiful

In this unit you'll learn that development is not just about big expensive projects. Small local projects can improve people's lives faster.

Ghana's water problem

◀ *Like a drink of this?*

This is Lamisi. And this is her family's water supply, for drinking, cooking and washing. She has been here collecting water for over three hours already.

The water in the bucket looks very muddy. But far worse than the mud are the things you can't see: bacteria that cause diarrhoea, typhoid, and cholera; and tiny eggs that grow into worms inside you, leading to bilharzia and other diseases.

Development little by little

Lamisi is not alone. Over 5 million Ghanaians have no access to clean safe water. One day everyone in Ghana will have piped water. But that could be years away. People can't wait. So, right now, many villages are digging wells for themselves with help from a UK charity called WaterAid. Everyone in the village gets involved:

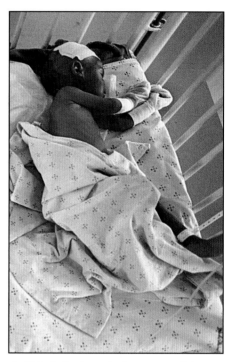

▲ *This baby has cholera, one of the many diseases caught from dirty water.*

> WaterAid supplies the know-how, the materials for lining the well, and the pump.

⬇

> Villagers form a committee to decide where the well will be, and organise the work.

⬇

> Everyone in the village joins in to help clear the site, and dig, and carry soil away.

⬇

> Some villagers are trained to look after the well and carry out repairs.

Cost of a hand-dug well: about £1200.
Cost of Akosombo dam: over £130 million (in 1960).

▲ *A new well. Everyone helped to build it, and everyone benefits.*

The difference a well makes

Wells don't bring just clean water!
When Abena (below) and other villagers were
asked how the wells had benefited them,
this list shows what they said.

The changes we noticed

- ☑ A more young people have time to go to school
- ☑ B teachers happier to stay in the villages to teach
- ☑ C much less illness, so less spent on medicine
- ☑ D women potters can produce more pots
- ☑ E more people cooking food to sell
- ☑ F more people selling iced water
- ☑ G no more quarrels with neighbouring villages about water
- ☑ H people take more pride in the village
- ☑ I cooked foods look much better
- ☑ J visitors can be offered clean drinking water
- ☑ K clothing and homes kept cleaner
- ☑ L much less time taken to fetch water
- ☑ M less far to walk for water, so less tired

Your turn

1 This diagram shows a hand-dug well, and pump.
 a Draw a larger simpler version of it.
 b Then write the labels below in the correct places.
 (There are just *some* leader lines to help you.)

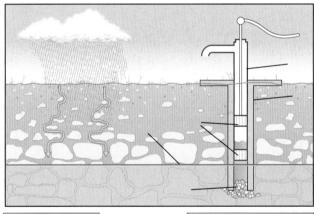

> rain soaks down to form groundwater

> the pump

> pushing the handle down draws water up the pipe

> the water table (the top of the groundwater)

> groundwater fills all the spaces in the rock

> hand-dug well lined with concrete and steel

> the water passes through valves in these plates

> soil and rock filter the water, helping to keep it clean

2 You are the chief of Lamisi's village. You plan to get
 a hand-dug well for your village.
 a Draw a large development compass rose and write
 in questions to help you think about your idea.
 For example two questions might be:
 How high is the water table here?
 Who will decide where the well will go?
 b Write in any answers you can, below your questions,
 in a different colour.

3 Now look at the list of changes **A–M** above.
 a Draw a larger copy of this diagram.

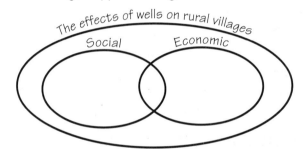

The effects of wells on rural villages
Social   Economic

 b Write letters **A–M** where you think they should go.
 (Glossary?) At least one where the loops overlap!
 c Choose one change that you placed in the overlap
 and explain why it belongs there.

4 These are all aspects of *sustainable* development:
 A Local people have a big say in the decision.
 B It benefits the local people.
 C It does not harm the environment.
 a Do you think the well in the photo on page 30 is a
 good example of sustainable development? Give it
 a score from 0–10.
 b Would you say it is a better example of sustainable
 development than the Akosombo dam (page 28)?
 c How many wells could have been dug for the price
 of the dam? (See the bottom of page 30.)

5 a Look at the title of this unit. What does it mean?
 b See if you can come up with a few more ideas for
 small projects that could make a big difference to
 Abena's village. (It's like the village on page 17.)
 c Choose the one you think the village would like
 most. How much do you think it would cost? Plan
 a campaign to raise money for it in your school.

Tackling the development gap

In this unit you'll learn about goals that world leaders have set, to help the poorer countries catch up.

A Happy New Millennium?

This is how our world looked at the start of the new millennium:

Happy New Millennium!

Happy for some...

1 January, 2000   **World population: 6 billion**

- 20% of the world's people barely survive (on less than $1 a day)
- 14% are undernourished
- 18% do not have access to safe water
- 40% do not have access to adequate toilets
- 8% of children die before age 5, most from preventable causes
- 20% of people aged over 15 can't read or write
- 17% of children of primary school age don't go to school
- 16% of all people are affected in some way by desertification

New resolutions for the New Millennium

In September 2000, world leaders held a **summit meeting**, to discuss the state of the world. They agreed a set of goals, to be met by the year 2015. Here are some of them:

We can do this...

...if we put our minds to it.

It's not rocket science!

The Millennium Development Goals

By 2015 we aim to:
- halve the % of people living on less than 1 dollar a day
- halve the % of undernourished people
- halve the % of people without access to a safe water supply
- cut under-5 deaths by two-thirds
- ensure that all children everywhere complete primary school
- make sure all development projects are sustainable
- reverse the damage to the environment

What about the money?

Meeting the above goals will cost an enormous amount of money. Where will it come from?

♦ The poorer countries don't have enough money.

♦ Governments of richer countries do give money each year to poorer countries, for development. (Around $56 billion in 2000.)

♦ Governments of richer countries have cancelled some debts of some poorer countries – which means these countries have more to spend.

♦ Ordinary people around the world also give money, through hundreds of **non-governmental organisations** (NGOs) such as Oxfam. We are giving lots through the *Make Poverty History* campaign, for example.

But experts say that meeting the Millennium Development Goals will cost around $100 billion a year – far more than is being given.

UNITED KINGDOM

▲ *The Prime Minister of the UK speaking at the Millennium Summit.*

Where could they get the extra money?

All around the world, people are putting pressure on world leaders to make sure the Millennium Development Goals are met. They say the extra money could be raised in these ways:

% of GNI given as aid in 2002

Australia	0.26
Canada	0.28
Denmark	0.96
France	0.38
Germany	0.27
Japan	0.23
Netherlands	0.81
Norway	0.89
United Kingdom	0.31
United States	0.13

1 Cancel *all* old Third World debt

This would free the LEDCs from a huge burden, and help them to make a fresh start.

2 Give more aid

Most rich countries do not give nearly as much aid as they had promised to give.

3 Make world trade fairer

This would help LEDCs to earn more, which they could then use for their own development.

You can find out more about making world trade fairer on page 86.

So can the goals be met?

Everyone hopes so – but it will take lots of careful planning and hard work, as well as money!

Talks about debt and fair trade go on, slowly. Meanwhile LEDCs get grants and loans to help them try to meet the goals. In 2004, Ghana got a grant of 19 million dollars from part of the World Bank, to start providing safe water and toilets for rural villages. Good news for Grace and her friends!

Your turn

1 It's the year 2000. Suppose the world is a village of 100 people. Using the statistics at the top of page 32, say how many of the 100 people:
   a are undernourished
   b have under a dollar a day to live on (for everything)
   c have no access to safe water
   d have no access to adequate toilets
   e are affected in some way by farmland turning to desert

2 Look at the Millennium Development Goals.
   a Why don't they aim for safe water for *everyone* by 2015?
   b Arrange the goals in what you think is their order of importance (most important first), and explain why you chose this order.
   c The cost of meeting these goals will be enormous. Give some reasons why.

3 Look at the table above. It shows the % of gross national income (GNI) that ten MEDCs gave as aid, in 2002.
   a What is *gross national income*? (Glossary?)
   b Draw a vertical scale like this one, and mark in the countries at the correct places.
   c They had promised to give 0.7% of GNI as aid. Mark in a dotted line at 0.7. How many had kept their promise?
   d Write a speech to make to the leaders of the other countries saying why they should give more aid. Make it as persuasive as you can.

4 a *'Local actions, global effects'.* What does that mean?
   b Do you think *your* actions could have any effect on world poverty? Explain.
   c Write down three things you could do to help ensure the Millennium Development Goals are met.

3 Earning a living

The big picture

This chapter is about changes in **economic activity** – what people do to earn a living. These are the big ideas behind the chapter:

◆ Economic activity falls into four sectors (as you saw in earlier books):
  primary – collecting things from the Earth and sea
  secondary – making or manufacturing things
  tertiary – providing services for people
  quaternary – high tech research

◆ The pattern of economic activity is always changing (even if slowly).

◆ An industry may grow large and important as demand for a product rises, and then decline because demand falls.

◆ An industry may also move away to countries where wages are lower.

◆ When an industry declines, or moves away, it causes problems for people and places.

◆ Regenerating an area takes a great deal of time, money and effort. The government usually has to step in to help.

Your goals for this chapter

By the end of this chapter you should be able to answer these questions:

◆ What do these terms mean, and what examples can I give for each ?

  primary sector   secondary sector   tertiary sector
  quaternary sector   heavy industry

◆ What does *employment structure* mean, and how has it changed in the UK over the centuries, and what is it like here today ?

◆ When and why did the coal industry grow very important, in the UK ? And why did it decline ?

◆ An industry can also move on from an area. Why might this happen ?

◆ In what ways can the decline or loss of an industry affect an area ?

◆ What kinds of things need to be done to regenerate an area ?

◆ What kinds of industries are important in the UK today ?

And then …

When you finish the chapter, come back to this page and see if you have met your goals !

Did you know?
◆ If you had lived 300 years ago, you'd probably have worked in farming.

Did you know?
◆ In 1950 nobody in the UK worked in IT. (There were no computers !)
◆ In 2000, 855 000 people had IT-related jobs.

Did you know?
◆ Manufacturing is in decline in the UK.
◆ Over 575 000 manufacturing jobs were lost in the period 1997–2004.

Did you know?
◆ 100 years ago, Britain was the world's top steel producer.
◆ Now China is top, and Britain does not produce much steel at all.

Your chapter starter

Look at the photo on page 34.

What is this man doing ?

Why is he doing it ?

Which employment sector is he in ? (… And what about the rabbit ?)

How do you think you'll earn your living, one day ?

No, the rabbit didn't mind a bit.

The changing pattern of economic activity

Here you'll see how the pattern of economic activity in Britain has changed over the centuries.

What kind of work do we do?

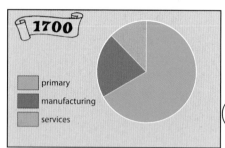

It's 1700 – and this shows the **employment structure** in Britain.

Most people work in the primary sector – mainly in farming.

The secondary sector is quite small by comparison …

… and the tertiary sector is the smallest.

Then the Industrial Revolution begins, and changes everything.

Britain begins to produce huge amounts of iron and steel …

… and turns them into trains, railways, ships, new machinery.

People flock into towns to work in the new factories.

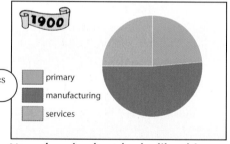

Now the pie chart looks like this. But it won't last! Soon …

… the key industries (coal, iron, steel, textiles) start to decline.

But the service sector keeps on growing and growing …

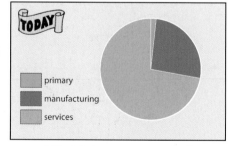

… and that brings us to today's employment structure.

But Britain is not alone. Most of the world's more developed countries have gone through similar changes.

Your turn

Page 36 will help you answer some of these questions.

Employment structure

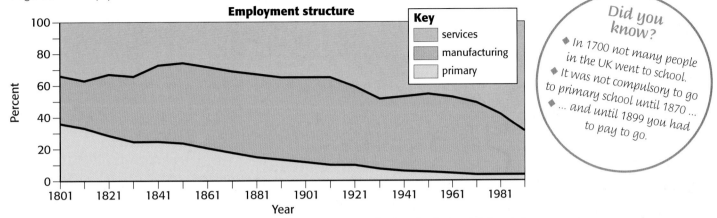

Key
- services
- manufacturing
- primary

1 What does *employment structure* mean? (Glossary.)

2 Look at the graph above. It is another way to show the changes described on page 36.
  By 1821, about what % of people were working:
  a in the primary sector? What did most of them do?
  b in the secondary sector? (You need to subtract!) Give three jobs they could have done.
  c in the tertiary sector? Give three jobs for these.

3 Now look at the overall shape of the graph.
  a Which sector has declined steadily since 1801?
  b Since this sector has declined so much, why are we not all starving? Give as many reasons as you can.
  c Which sector has grown most, overall?

4 a In which sector did employment grow fastest between 1801 and 1851?
  b Suggest a reason for this.
  c Give reasons why this sector shrank overall, in the 20th century.
  d Since this sector has shrunk so much, why have we not run out of things to buy?

5 Now think about how life in Britain has changed.
  a This spider map sums up Britain in 1700. Make your own copy and add *at least three* more key facts. (Could be things you know from history.)

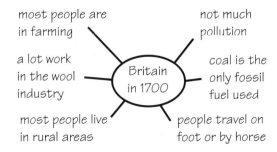

most people are in farming

not much pollution

a lot work in the wool industry

Britain in 1700

coal is the only fossil fuel used

most people live in rural areas

people travel on foot or by horse

  b Now do a similar spider map for Britain in 1850.
  c And finally, do the same for Britain today.

6 During the Industrial Revolution many towns grew fast. Manchester was one. This shows it around 1850. Look at all the tall factory chimneys.

The development compass rose (page 7) helps you think up questions about how and why places change, and the consequences of change.
  a Draw a *large* copy of the DCR below.

Manchester in 1850

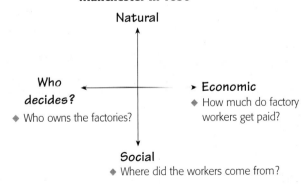

Natural

Who decides?
- Who owns the factories?

Economic
- How much do factory workers get paid?

Social
- Where did the workers come from?

  b On your DCR, write in *at least* 8 more questions you could ask about Manchester in 1850, using the picture to help you.

The rise and fall of the coal industry

In this unit you'll explore how an industry can grow big and important – and then decline. We take the British coal industry as our example.

An island built on coal

Coal has been mined in Britain for at least 2000 years. We can tell this from some ancient flint axes that were found stuck in lumps of coal. The Romans learned about coal when they arrived here, and kept stores of it along Hadrian's Wall for fires for their soldiers.

Britain has a lot of coal. That made the Industrial Revolution possible! Coal was needed to extract iron from iron ore (in the form of coke), and to fuel the steam engines that pulled the iron trains and drove the new machinery in factories.

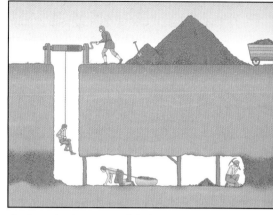

▲ A coal mine around 1700.

A map of Britain's coal deposits

This map shows Britain's coal deposits. Over the last 150 years there were around 1200 working **collieries**, with deep coal mines. Now there are less than 10.

At its peak, the coal industry employed over a million people. When a colliery closed there was often no other work in the area, so it was a disaster.

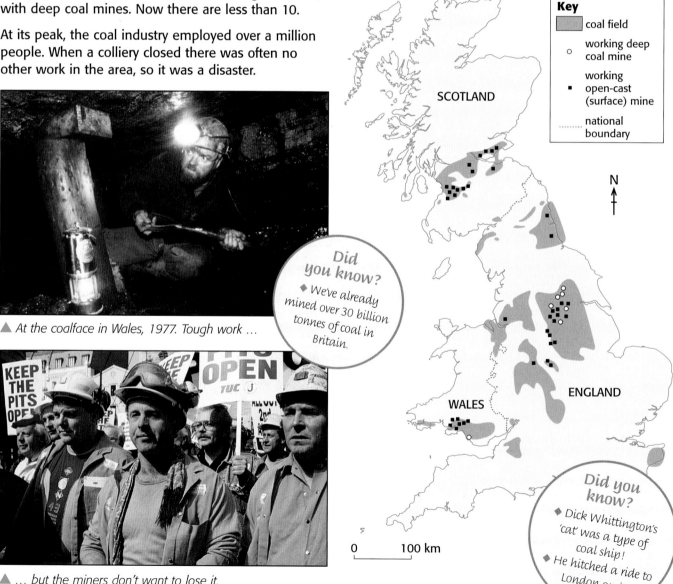

▲ At the coalface in Wales, 1977. Tough work …

▲ … but the miners don't want to lose it.

Key

▨ coal field

○ working deep coal mine

■ working open-cast (surface) mine

‥‥ national boundary

SCOTLAND

N

WALES

ENGLAND

Did you know?
♦ We've already mined over 30 billion tonnes of coal in Britain.

Did you know?
♦ Dick Whittington's 'cat' was a type of coal ship!
♦ He hitched a ride to London on it.

0   100 km

Your turn

1 In which parts of Britain is coal found?
Imagine you are telling someone who has no map
to look at. Make your answer very clear.

2 What is a *colliery*?

3 Look at the drawing and first photo on page 38.
Do you think miners had a tough job?
What problems might they have faced?
You could give your answer as a spider map.

4 Now explain what's going on in the second photo.

5 Why did the coal industry decline? Time to find out!
You'll start by drawing a *large* graph using the data
in the table on the right. (Use a full page.)
  a First, draw axes like those started on the far right.
  b Plot the data.
  c Join the points with a smooth curve. No ruler!
  d Give your graph a title.

6 Your next task is to **annotate** (add notes to) your
graph using the fact box below. Use neat writing and
keep your notes brief. Don't just copy the facts.

7 Now look at the things you've noted on your graph.
  a Underline in one colour any that you think will lead
  to a *rise in demand* for coal. (Glossary?)
  b Underline in a different colour any you think would
  lead to a *fall in demand*. Add a key for your colours.
  c i About when did production reach its peak?
    ii About how much coal was mined that year?
  d Coal production fell between 1910 and 1920, then
  rose again. See if you can think of a reason.

Coal production in Britain

Year	Coal production (millions of tons)
1750	5
1800	10
1830	31
1840	43
1850	63
1860	88
1870	116
1880	147
1890	182
1900	225
1910	265
1920	230
1930	244
1940	224
1950	204
1960	186
1970	135
1980	105
1990	88
1996	40
2000	22

Did you know?
- The UK still has enough coal to last hundreds of years.
- But our oil and gas could run out within 20 years.

Did you know?
- The UK's coal industry is almost gone ...
- ... but China's coal industry is booming!

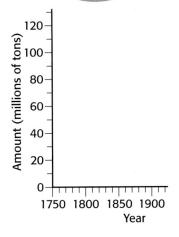

FACT BOX

1885 In Germany Mr Benz develops the first petrol-driven car.

1823 The first public railway (the Stockton and Darlington Railway) opens – with steam engines.

1782 James Watt develops a steam engine that can drive machinery. Coal is used to boil the water.

1813 The first gasworks built, in London, making **town gas** (from coal) to light homes.

1850 By now Britain is producing over half the world's iron.

1900 The UK's first power station opens, with coal as fuel. People rush to get electric lights in.

1859 The world's first oil well is drilled in America.

1913 1 128 000 men are employed in coal mining.

1965 Gas is discovered in the North Sea.

1967 The switch of homes from town gas to North Sea gas begins.

1956 The 'Clean Air Act' bans the burning of smoky coal in open fires in homes.

1992 There are now 58 000 miners.

1956 The UK's first **nuclear** power station opens.

2000 About 9000 miners left.

1896 The UK's first car factory is set up in Coventry. Cars use petrol, not coal – so oil is imported.

1969 Oil is discovered in the North Sea.

1965 By now many mines have closed down. (Some exhausted, others losing money.)

1970 By now imported coal is cheaper than UK coal!

1984 Miners go on strike for almost a year, to protest against pit closures.

1992 Power stations are switching from coal to gas – cleaner and cheaper.

1930 More and more oil is being imported – for cars *and* factories!

When an industry declines

Here you'll explore how the decline in an industry can affect an area – and see how people in one coal village are fighting back.

Another depressing day for Joe

It's 10 am on 1 December, 1994. Joe should get up – but for what? It's over 8 months since the Ollerton colliery closed, putting 1000 people out of work. Including him.

He drags himself out of bed. And looks out the window, as he does every day, at the ugly scar where the mine is. It lies gloomy and silent, an ever-present reminder of how his life has changed.

Today he'll sign on the dole again. He'll look for a job on the noticeboard. But inside, he has no hope. Everyone is chasing the same few jobs. And who wants a person of nearly 40 who has only ever worked down the pit?.

He looks around. The house needs painting and the roof needs repairs. But he's worried about spending the money. His savings are going too fast already. His wife's part-time job pays very little. Soon it will be Christmas – not much fun for the children this year.

A long day lies ahead. He could call in on some friends. But he doesn't really like talking to people, these days. He feels useless, and trapped.

The legacy of decline

Joe is not alone. Between 1975 and 1995, nearly 300 000 miners lost their jobs, as the collieries closed down one by one.

Imagine what it's like when thousands of jobs are lost in an area, year after year.

- People may not be able to find other paid work.
- They may not have the right skills for new jobs.
- They won't have much money to spend.
- Many will suffer from stress and depression.
- Low morale will affect everyone in the family, even young people at school.
- Crime is likely to rise.
- The whole area will begin to look run down. (And a mining area is already polluted and scarred.)

But Joe is lucky, as you'll see on the next page. The people of Ollerton decided they would not let these things happen to them.

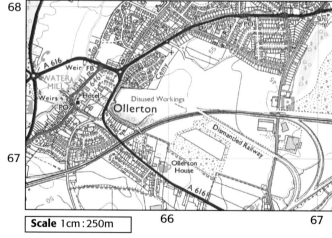

▲ *Ollerton colliery. The OS map below was made after it shut down. Can you match* ● *on the photo to a grid reference on the map?*

Scale 1cm : 250m

▶ *At the end of a shift in the Ollerton colliery.*

Ollerton fights back

The people of Ollerton were devastated when their pit closed. They held meetings to decide what to do. And in 1995 they formed a plan. They would:

◆ buy the land the mine was on, from British Coal

◆ get the site cleaned up

◆ build a new 'village' on it, with homes, businesses and open spaces.

They decided to call it **Sherwood Energy Village**. It would be a model for sustainablity. It would:

◆ use electricity only from renewable sources (wind, and organic waste such as wood chips)

◆ be designed to save as much energy as possible

◆ have businesses that do not harm the environment

◆ provide jobs to replace the 1000 that were lost.

How far has it got ?

The people formed a society to 'own' the village. (It was made up of local people and supporters.)

They bought the land for £50 000. And got a grant of £4 million from the government and European Union, to clean it up ready for building.

By 2004 some factories were completed. In 2005 work started on 186 new homes. The profit they make from selling these homes will be used to develop other things – such as play areas and sports facilities.

▲ New homes planned for Sherwoood Energy Village.

new homes

▲ Sherwood Energy Village underway in 2004, on the site of the old colliery. Some new factories are already in place. One corner of the site will be used for homes.

Your turn

1 When a big employer like a colliery closes, what other local businesses are likely to suffer ? (Clothes shops ? Pubs ?) You could give your answer as a spider map.

2 The seven bullet points on page 40 give some of the effects on a local area when a big employer closes.

  a Draw seven boxes in a circle, as shown here – but use a full page, and make each box big enough to take a few words.

  b In each box, summarise one bullet point. For the first one you could write: *No paid work*.

  c i Now pick out any boxes giving *economic* effects. Colour their edges in one colour.

    ii Use another colour for *social* effects.

    iii Use a third colour for *enviromental* effects.

    iv Add a colour key in the corner of your page.

  d Do you think there's a link between *Low morale* and *No paid work* ? If you think so, link those two boxes with a curved arrow. Which end should the arrow head go on ?

  e Join other boxes you think should be linked, in the same way. (Some lines may need an arrow head at each end.)

  f Give your drawing a suitable title.

3 Now think about the positive effects the Sherwood Energy Village is likely to have. List them under three headings: *Economic*, *Social* and *Environmental*.

4 Which do *you* think is better for Ollerton – a working colliery, or the Sherwood Energy Village ? Give as many reasons as you can to support your answer.

5 You're Joe. It's the year 2012. Write a piece for the *Ollerton Weekly* about how the Sherwood Energy Village transformed your life.

Today's industries

SCOTLAND

Here you'll learn about some of the industries that are important in the UK today. We use Scotland as example.

Out with the old, in with the new

When old industries die, new ones grow. It has happened over and over again, through the centuries.

This map shows the population density of Scotland. Look at the strip where most people live. It's in Scotland's coal area! Check on the map on page 38.

Once, heavy industry thrived in this area: coal, steel, and shipbuilding. When these declined, thousands of people were left without work. Scotland suffered badly. Many people were forced to leave and look for work elsewhere.

But today, Scotland has lots of new businesses.

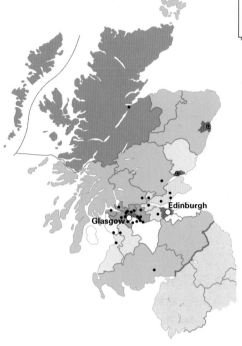

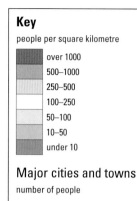

Key

people per square kilometre

	over 1000
	500–1000
	250–500
	100–250
	50–100
	10–50
	under 10

Major cities and towns

number of people

○	400 000–1 000 000
◉	100 000–400 000
•	25 000–100 000

Some of Scotland's key industries

These are all important to Scotland today:

Electronic goods 29% of Europe's electronic notebooks, and over 7% of the world's PCs, are made in Scotland.

Software Dozens of companies work in software design – for computer games, and mobile phones, and other uses.

Life sciences A lot of advanced medical research goes on in Scotland, and many big drug companies have bases here.

Financial services Two of Europe's top banks are Scottish. Many big insurance and pension companies are based here.

Call centres In 2004, 56 000 people worked in call centres in Scotland, taking calls on behalf of banks and other companies.

Tourism Scotland expects this to keep growing. Around 200 000 people (or 9% of the workforce) are in jobs related to tourism.

How do new industries grow ?

When an industry declines, it takes bright ideas, and hard work, and money, to attract new sources of employment to the area.

The area may get grants to train people in new skills, and improve roads and other facilities. This will help it attract new companies.

A government body called **Scottish Development International** works hard to attract companies from outside the UK.

Some companies are attracted to Scotland, or start there, because research going on in Scottish universities will benefit them.

Then, if a new company is successful, it often attracts similar companies. (So Scotland has clusters of companies working in the medical field.)

What about the rest of the UK ?

It's the same story. The industries on page 42 are important elsewhere in the UK too. The government and EU give grants to help many areas. And all parts of the UK try to attract companies from other countries.

But it's not all good news

It is not all good news. The UK can't relax !

◆ Steel-making and shipbuilding declined because steel and ships could be made more cheaply in other countries. The industries just moved on.

◆ It's the same today. Many foreign companies set up here with the help of grants – and then move on to countries where wages are lower. (Some companies have already moved on from Scotland.)

◆ Even British companies move jobs to other countries with lower wages. For example many have moved their call centres to India.

▲ *Bad news day: in 2001 Motorola closed this mobile phone factory in Scotland, after just ten years.*

Your turn

1 The government gives grants to attract companies to set up in the UK.
   a Complete this consequence map to show how that could benefit an area. (Add lots more boxes.)

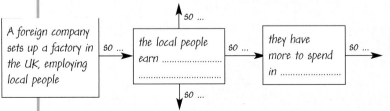

   b In what ways might it benefit the government? (See if you can do a consequence map for this?)

2 The industries that are most likely to move to other countries are those that need a lot of workers for repetitive jobs.
   a Explain why.
   b Look at page 42. Which two of the jobs shown here may be most at risk? Explain your choice.

3 *'New inventions lead to new industries. In time these may move on.'*
   Draw a strip cartoon to show this. Take the computer chip as your example – invented in 1958, when our heavy industries were in decline.

4 *'We should accept lower pay, to keep our industries.'*
   Do you agree? Write an article for a newspaper, giving your opinion. Suggest other options if you can.

4 ◄ Focus on France

Welcome to France. Just twenty minutes from the UK by tunnel. Where you'll find …

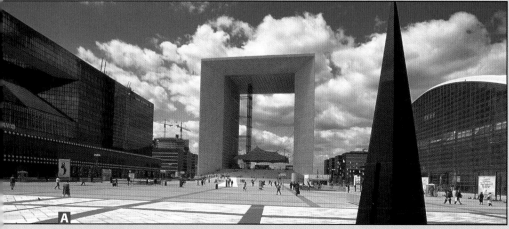

A … *gleaming new developments …*

B ▲ … *famous monuments …*

C ▲ … *vineyards …*

D ▲ … *glamorous Mediterranean beaches …*

G ▲ … *and some great places to go skiing.*

E ▲ … *hundreds of small rural villages …*   **F** ▲ … *lots of outdoor markets …*

The big picture

This chapter is about France. These are the big ideas behind the chapter:

◆ France is one of the world's most prosperous and developed countries.

◆ Like every country, it has a unique set of physical features, climate zones, and natural resources.

◆ These lead to patterns of population distribution and economic activity.

◆ Like every country, it faces problems. Solving them needs planning and management.

◆ France and other countries are interdependent. It needs them, and vice versa!

Your goals for this chapter

By the end of this chapter you should be able to answer these questions:

◆ Which are the main relief features of France, and what are its four main rivers called?

◆ What is its climate like, and why?

◆ How is its population spread around France, and what factors have influenced the pattern? (Give at least four factors.)

◆ Which kinds of things helped to make France prosperous? (Give at least four.)

◆ Where are the main areas of industry in France?

◆ How is the pattern of industry changing, and why?

◆ In what other ways is the economy changing? (Give at least two ways.)

◆ What does *rural depopulation* mean, and what are some of its causes, and consequences?

◆ Why did Paris face problems by 1970, and how did it tackle them?

◆ What's Marne-la-Vallée like? (Make at least five statements about it.)

◆ In what ways are France and other countries interdependent? (Give at least five.)

And then ...

When you finish this chapter you can come back to this page and see if you have met your goals!

Did you know?

◆ England and France have often been at war.
◆ The longest was the Hundred Years' War, which Edward III began in 1337.

Did you know?

◆ 8000 years ago, England and France were joined.
◆ Then rising seas and floods caused a split.
◆ And then we built a tunnel ...

Did you know?

◆ Mary Queen of Scots became Queen of France when she was just 17.

Did you know?

◆ England 'owned' Calais for over 200 years, until 1558 ...
◆ ... and the English still like to go shopping there.

Your chapter starter

What's the first thing that springs to mind, when you think of France?

In what ways is France like the UK?

In what ways is it different from the UK?

France gets more tourists than any other country in the world. Why do you think that is? Come up with as many reasons as you can.

C'est magnifique!

A little physical geography

Here you will find out about the main physical features of France, and its climate.

The main physical features of France

This map shows the **relief** – and the four main rivers.

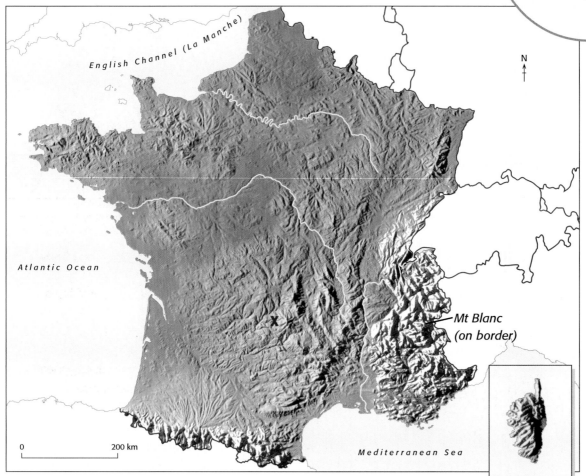

English Channel (La Manche)

N

Atlantic Ocean

X

Mt Blanc (on border)

0   200 km

Mediterranean Sea

Look at those great mountain ranges in the south east and south west. They were created when the African plate pushed north into the Eurasian plate, causing rock to fold upwards. And the high land around **X** is made up of extinct volcanoes!

▲ *One of the extinct volcanoes around **X** on the map above.*

▲ *On the north coast of France. What landforms can you see?*

The climate in France

Some of France has much the same climate as the UK.
But some of it gets a lot warmer, as this map shows.

Key

Overall, quite like much of the UK; quite mild in winter and warm in summer; quite a lot of rain all year, especially in the higher areas.

Overall, much warmer than the UK; hot and very dry in summer; very mild winters with some rain.

Cold or very cold all year round; precipitation often in the form of snow.

Gets hot quickly in summer and cold quickly in winter; quite a bit of rain.

Quite cool all year, and cold in winter; a lot of rain in the higher areas.

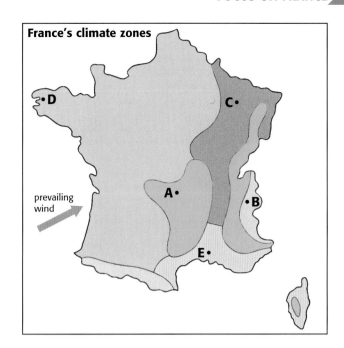

France's climate zones

prevailing wind

Your turn

1 France is sometimes called *Le Hexagon*. Why?
2 The map opposite shows *relief*. What does that mean?
3 This sketch map shows the main physical features of France, plus its capital city.

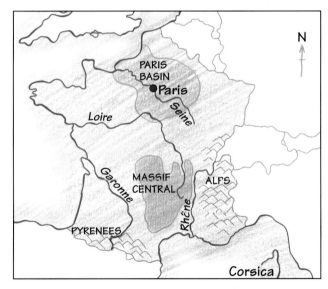

Your job is to copy and complete these sentences, using words and phrases from the box on the right. (You may need to use some more than once.) Use the maps on pages 46 and 129 for clues.

a France has got ___ very high mountain ranges. The Pyrenees separate France from ___ . The ___ separate it from ____ and ____ .

b The Massif Central is an ____ area, but not as high as the ____ or ____ .

c The Paris basin is an area of ___ ___ around Paris.

d The Rhône rises in the _____ in _____ and flows to the _____ _____ .

e The _____ rises in the _____ _____ and flows to the _____ _____ .

f The _____ is France's longest river.

g Paris is on the River _____ .

h The _____ and _____ are fed by melting glaciers.

i The _____ named Corsica is part of France. It is in the _____ _____ .

j Overall, the ___ and ____ of France have low land.

4 Now look at the climate map above.

a What does the word *climate* mean? (Glossary?)

b Say what the climate is like at each of these places and then try to explain why. (The maps on page 46 and 129 will help.)
  i at A   ii at B   iii at C   iv at D   v at E

5 And finally, write a summary for yourself about France's physical geography and climate – in a form that you think will *really* help you remember! (Would an annotated sketch map work for you?)

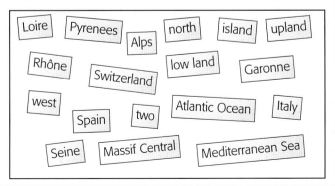

Loire Pyrenees Alps north island upland
Rhône Switzerland low land Garonne
west Spain two Atlantic Ocean Italy
Seine Massif Central Mediterranean Sea

So where is everyone?

Here you'll see how the population of France is spread around, and explore reasons for the pattern.

Population distribution in France

France has about the same number of people as the UK – but it's a much larger country, as this table shows:

	France	UK
Population (millions)	60	60
Area (sq km)	550000	242000

Like the UK, France is divided into regions. The map on the right shows the 22 regions, and their French names.

The map below, that looks like pizza, shows how the population is spread. The more red, the more crowded! The five largest cities are named, plus a few others.

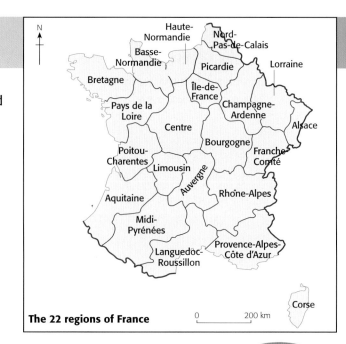

The 22 regions of France

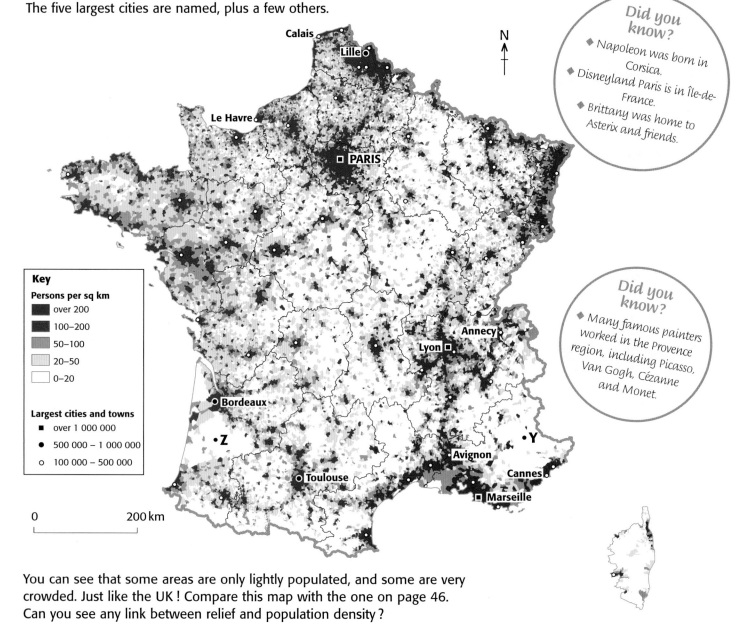

Key

Persons per sq km

- over 200
- 100–200
- 50–100
- 20–50
- 0–20

Largest cities and towns

- ■ over 1 000 000
- ● 500 000 – 1 000 000
- ○ 100 000 – 500 000

0   200 km

Did you know?
- Napoleon was born in Corsica.
- Disneyland Paris is in Île-de-France.
- Brittany was home to Asterix and friends.

Did you know?
- Many famous painters worked in the Provence region, including Picasso, Van Gogh, Cézanne and Monet.

You can see that some areas are only lightly populated, and some are very crowded. Just like the UK! Compare this map with the one on page 46. Can you see any link between relief and population density?

People on the move

The population distribution in a country is always changing, because people are always on the move ! Many **migrate** from one part of a country to another.

Look at this map. It shows the overall trends in migration in France between 1990 and 2000.

These are some of the reasons people move:

◆ job loss in areas where industry is in decline

◆ growth of new industries and new jobs in other areas

◆ the attractions of a different climate or lifestyle.

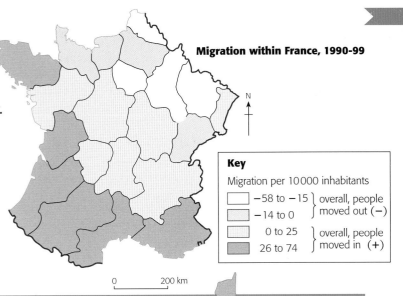

Migration within France, 1990-99

Key

Migration per 10 000 inhabitants

☐	−58 to −15	overall, people moved out (−)
☐	−14 to 0	
☐	0 to 25	overall, people moved in (+)
☐	26 to 74	

0   200 km

Your turn

1 First, compare France and the UK. Using the table at the top of page 48 to help you, copy this paragraph, and fill in the blanks from the list in italics.

France is over _____ the size of the UK. But their populations are _____. This means France is _____ crowded. It has _____ people per square km on average, while the UK has _____ .

equal   9166   248   half   2.27   very
109   three times   too   twice   less   4033

2 This question is about the regions of France. Name:

a the region that contains Paris

b the region nearest the UK

c a region in the Massif Central

d one that offers beach holidays – and winter skiing

e a region bordering Spain and the Atlantic Ocean

f the one that juts out furthest into the Atlantic Ocean

g one that juts out into Germany

3 This is about population density. Write out each statement. Then, if it's true, tick it. If false, correct it !

A Île-de-France is the most crowded region of France.

B Alsace is much less crowded than Auvergne.

C Very few people live along the Mediterranean coast.

D Overall, central France is the most populous part.

E The city of Lille is part of a conurbation.

4 So why is the population distributed this way ? Using the maps on pages 46, 47, and 52, and your own bright ideas, see if you can explain why:

a no-one lives at Y on the map on page 48

b the area around Z is lightly populated

c a large area around Paris is very heavily populated

d the area around Lille is heavily populated

e Alsace is heavily populated

f Marseille has grown to be a large flourishing city

g population density tends to be high along the coast.

5 More detective work ! The map on page 46 shows the four longest rivers in France.

a Compare the routes of these rivers with the map of population density. What do you notice ? Aha ?

b Suggest a way to check this more carefully.

c Now give reasons to explain what you noticed.

6 This table shows the five largest French metropolitan areas, and the three largest British ones (to compare).

Population of top metropolitan areas in 2004 (millions)			
Birmingham	3.20	Lyon	1.68
Leeds	1.49	Marseille	1.55
Lille	1.14	Paris	11.42
London	11.26	Toulouse	0.99

a What does *metropolitan area* mean ? (Glossary)

b Draw a horizontal bar chart to show this data (one colour for French places, another for British).

c Compare Paris with the next largest metropolitan area in France. How many times larger is it ?

d Repeat **c** for London and Birmingham.

e About what % of the country's population lives:
i in and around Paris ? **ii** in and around London ?

f Which capital appears to dominate its country more, London or Paris ?

7 Now, migration. (The map on page 52 will help here.)

a From the map above, which was the main direction of migration in France, in the period 1990–1999?
i from north to south   **ii** from west to east

b Nord-pas-de-Calais and Lorraine are two of the regions that lost most people. Suggest reasons.

c Île-de-France also lost people. Suggest reasons why people might want to move from that area.

d Provence-Alpes-Cote d'Azur is one region that gained people. Suggest reasons why someone from Nord-pas-de-Calais might want to move here.

An overview of the French economy

In this unit you'll learn some of the reasons why France is so prosperous.

One of the world's most developed countries ...

France is one of the world's most prosperous and developed countries.
How did it turn out like this?
There are many reasons. We'll look at three groups of reasons here.

1 Natural resources

Resources are things we need to live, or can use to earn a living.
France is *not* very rich in natural resources. But it makes the most of them!

Fertile soil

- Fertile soil is one thing France has plenty of. Over half the land is fertile.
- In the past, the wealth from farming helped to fund new industries.
- Today farming, and the food industries based on it, are still very important.
- The main crops are cereals (mainly wheat), sugar beet, grapes for wine, fruit, and vegetables.
- Livestock is important too: cattle, sheep, goats, pigs, chickens – and rabbits!

Metal ores

- France has large deposits of iron ore. It used this to make the machines for its new factories, during its Industrial Revolution.
- But the iron ore is low grade. So it's not mined any longer. France now imports the iron ore it uses to make steel.
- There's also quite a lot of bauxite (aluminium ore). France is one of Europe's top aluminium producers.

Sources of energy

France is not rich in sources of energy.

- It had some coal, which fuelled its Industrial Revolution (as in the UK).
- But the coal industry has declined, as in the UK. The last French coal mine closed in 2004.
- It has a little oil and gas – but not nearly enough. So it has to import these.
- It has some uranium ore, so it chose to develop nuclear power. Now nearly 80% of its electricity comes from nuclear power stations like this one:

- It also uses several of its rivers for hydroelectricity.

Climate and landscape

- In most of France the climate is good for crops.
- The climate also attracts tourists – and tourism is one of France's top industries.
- The French landscape also attracts them – beaches, mountains, forests, and peaceful rural scenes. (Over 20% of France is forested.)

The sea

- The sea means a busy French fishing industry.
- It also means ports for exporting and importing!

2 Geographical location

◆ Trade with other countries usually helps to make a country wealthy. So having a coast, and close neighbours, has helped France.

◆ Being near the UK helped it in one special way. The Industrial Revolution began here and spread to France. (But it was not so dramatic in France. French industry grew fastest after World War II.)

3 Policies

◆ Like Britain, France colonised other countries. See the map on page 60. The materials it took from them helped to make France rich.

◆ France was one of the founders of the European Union, and is a leading member. It has benefited greatly from the EU.

◆ The French government has always played a big part in the economy. It still owns, or partly owns, several key industries.

▲ The French government has a big share in some big companies - so it can boss them around!

The economy is still changing

Every economy changes. These are the main changes in France.

◆ Agriculture is still very important – but the number of farmers, and small farms, is falling. Big farms with lots of machinery are taking over. (The government encourages this.)

◆ Traditional industries like mining, steelmaking, shipbuilding and textiles are in decline. (But not as much as in the UK.)

◆ Modern industries are flourishing – mainly the car industry, aerospace industry (planes and rockets), pharmaceutical drugs, and electronics.

◆ Most industry used to be in the old coal areas, and around Paris. The government has been helping new factories to start up in different regions, to help the poorer areas.

◆ As in the UK, the service sector is growing.

You'll take a closer look at the economy in the next unit.

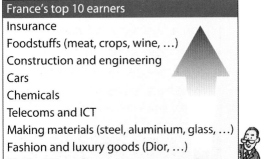

France's top 10 earners

Insurance
Foodstuffs (meat, crops, wine, ...)
Construction and engineering
Cars
Chemicals
Telecoms and ICT
Making materials (steel, aluminium, glass, ...)
Fashion and luxury goods (Dior, ...)
Medical drugs
Tourism
Aerospace (planes, rockets)

Ça, c'est 11!

Your turn

1 Natural resources lead to jobs! For example:

fertile soil → growing grapes → making wine → selling wine

At each stage of the chain, more wealth is created. See if you can give five more examples for France. (Not all starting with soil – and some can be shorter.)

2 Now look at your chains for **1**. Underline the primary sector jobs in one colour, the secondary in another, and the tertiary in a third. (Glossary?)

3 Look at the table on the right below. The structure of employment is changing in France, just as in the UK.

  a Turn to the graph for the UK at the top of page 37, to see how it was drawn.

  b Now draw a similar graph for France, using this table. Join the points with a smooth curve.

  c Compare the two graphs. In what ways are they similar? In what ways are they different?

4 On page 50 it says France is one of the world's most developed and prosperous countries. So how does it compare with the UK? Look at these figures for 2002:

	GDP per capita (US$ PPP)	Life expectancy	Doctors per 100 000 people	HDI
France	26 920	79	330	0.932
UK	26 150	78	164	0.936

  a Which country appears to be more developed? Did you have any problems in deciding? If so, why?

  b Suggest three other questions you could ask about the two countries, to check your conclusion in **a**.

Year	1970	1980	1990	2000
Primary (%)	13	8	6	4
Secondary (%)	38	35	29	25
Tertiary (%)	49	57	66	71

A closer look at the French economy

In this unit you'll see how economic activity is spread around France – and how it varies from region to region.

What goes on where?

This simplified map shows economic activity across France. The regions are numbered. You will find their names in the table on page 53.

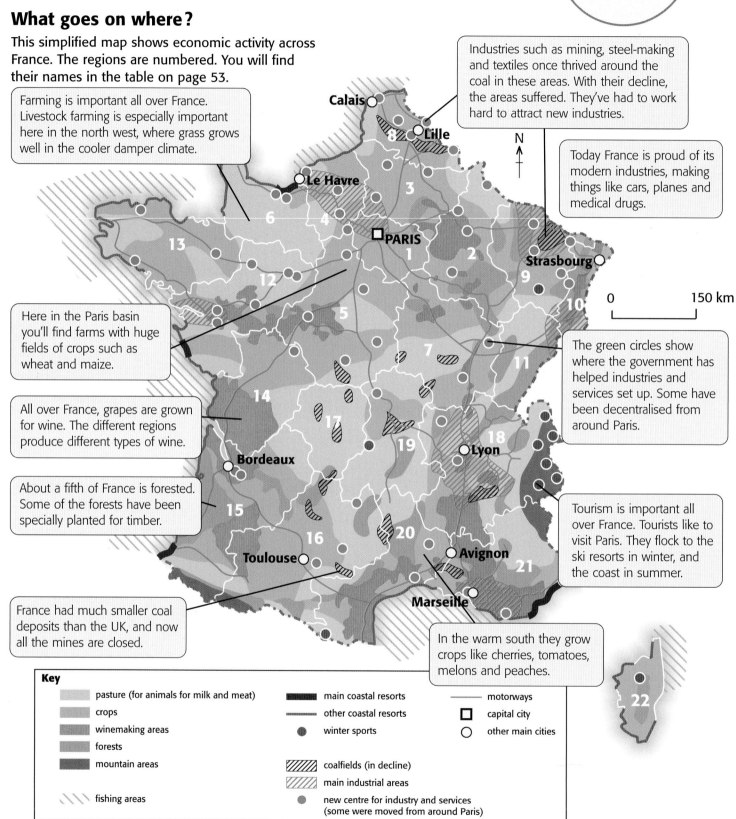

Farming is important all over France. Livestock farming is especially important here in the north west, where grass grows well in the cooler damper climate.

Industries such as mining, steel-making and textiles once thrived around the coal in these areas. With their decline, the areas suffered. They've had to work hard to attract new industries.

Today France is proud of its modern industries, making things like cars, planes and medical drugs.

Here in the Paris basin you'll find farms with huge fields of crops such as wheat and maize.

All over France, grapes are grown for wine. The different regions produce different types of wine.

About a fifth of France is forested. Some of the forests have been specially planted for timber.

The green circles show where the government has helped industries and services set up. Some have been decentralised from around Paris.

Tourism is important all over France. Tourists like to visit Paris. They flock to the ski resorts in winter, and the coast in summer.

France had much smaller coal deposits than the UK, and now all the mines are closed.

In the warm south they grow crops like cherries, tomatoes, melons and peaches.

Calais, Lille, Le Havre, PARIS, Strasbourg, Bordeaux, Lyon, Toulouse, Avignon, Marseille

0   150 km

Key

pasture (for animals for milk and meat)	main coastal resorts
crops	other coastal resorts
winemaking areas	winter sports
forests	
mountain areas	
fishing areas	

motorways
□ capital city
○ other main cities

coalfields (in decline)
main industrial areas
new centre for industry and services (some were moved from around Paris)

It's different from region to region

In every country, economic activity varies from region to region. So does the wealth that's produced! This table shows changes across France.

One economic problem

One problem that has troubled France for many years is high unemployment. Often, more than 1 person in 10 is out of work.

So in 2000, the government ordered the working week to be cut from 39 to 35 hours per person, to give more people the chance to work.

But by 2004 it was clear that this had not helped to cut unemployment. Now the government is looking for other ways to solve the problem.

	Region	% of France's total GDP it produces	% of working population in agric.	% of working population in industry	% of working population in services
1	Île-de-France	28.4	0.5	18.7	80.8
2	Champagne-Ardenne	2.1	8.6	25.0	66.4
3	Picardie	2.7	4.9	29.1	65.9
4	Haute-Normandie	2.8	1.9	29.2	68.9
5	Centre	3.8	4.7	29.9	65.4
6	Basse-Normandie	2.1	9.4	24.9	65.7
7	Bourgogne	2.5	6.0	27.4	66.6
8	Nord-Pas-de-Calais	5.4	1.9	27.1	71.0
9	Lorraine	3.4	2.8	30.2	67.0
10	Alsace	3.1	2.4	33.4	64.2
11	Franche-Compté	1.7	4.7	35.5	59.8
12	Pays de la Loire	4.8	6.2	29.0	64.7
13	Bretagne	4.1	7.6	25.3	67.0
14	Poitou-Charentes	2.2	8.4	24.0	67.6
15	Aquitaine	4.4	7.5	21.3	71.2
16	Midi-Pyrénées	3.8	5.9	24.4	69.7
17	Limousin	1.0	9.2	24.4	66.3
18	Rhône-Alpes	9.7	4.1	28.0	67.7
19	Auvergne	1.8	8.1	28.4	63.5
20	Languedoc-Roussillon	3.0	6.9	18.1	75.0
21	Provence-Alpes-Côte d'Azur	6.8	3.0	17.9	79.0
22	Corse	0.34	5.7	15.6	78.7
	Average for France	**100%**	**3.2**	**24.5**	**72.3**

Your turn

1 Look at the map on page 52. It has been greatly simplified, to help you see the overall pattern.

  a First, farming. Name one region of France where you are likely to find:
    i crops of fruit and vegetables
    ii large fields full of wheat and sugar beet
    iii large herds of dairy cattle (for milk).
  b Now look at the wine-growing areas. Are they all clustered together or spread out? Write a paragraph saying what you notice.

2 a i The north east of France has traditionally been an industrial area. Suggest a reason for this.
    ii What kinds of problems might it be having now?
  b Write a paragraph summarising where the main industrial areas are, in France today.
  c The map shows some *decentralised* industries.
    i What does that term mean?
    ii Who caused them to decentralise, and why?

3 Now look at the table at the top of this page. *GDP or gross domestic product* is the total wealth produced in a country in a year.
  a Which region of France contributes most wealth to the economy? Give reasons. (Page 52 will help.)
  b Which contributes least? Suggest reasons.
  c In which region is the % of the population working in agriculture: i largest? ii smallest?
  d In which region is the % of the population working in industry: i largest? ii smallest?

Employment structure for three French regions

i   ii   iii

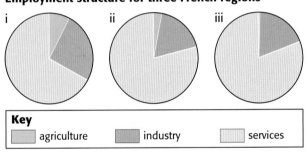

Key
  agriculture   industry   services

4 The pie charts above show employment structure in:
  a Île-de-France
  b Bretagne
  c Provence-Alpes-Côte d'Azur
  But they're mixed up! Match each to its correct region.

5 This describes one of France's regions. Which one? (Look back at earlier units for clues.)

  ◆ hot dry sunny summers
  ◆ lots of people have moved here, or come here on holiday – partly for the sun!
  ◆ lots of vineyards
  ◆ no very big cities (of over 500 000 people)
  ◆ a smaller % of its population work in industry than for most other regions

6 a Close your eyes, and pick a region from the table above. (If you get the one in question 5, try again!)
  b Using 5 as an example, write a set of clues for it.
  c Now ask your partner to identify the region.

Rural depopulation

In this unit you'll explore one of France's problems: the migration of people out of rural areas. We take a village in Auvergne as example.

Letter from Langy

Le Bourg
03150 Langy
Auvergne

Mercredi

Ma chère Suzanne

So much has happened since I got your letter. We bought a new house at last !!! And this is my very first letter from Langy, right in the middle of France. Well, it's not exactly a new house. In fact over 100 years old and rather petite – here's a photo. But I really love it.

Langy is just a little village. With our arrival, the population went up to 201. An old man I met yesterday said it had been quite lively once, with a lot more people. It even had a shop – which closed after the war! The poor old primary school hung on for ages with only a handful of pupils, but finally gave up. It's the same with the church. Now it's used only for baptisms, weddings and funerals, and you have to get the key from one of our neighbours. As for transport – you could not manage without a car.

▲ Jacqueline's new house (on the right).

All this explains why the house was so cheap. I still can't believe how cheap, compared with Île de France. We saw some farmhouses further out that were almost falling down, and even cheaper. Some in the middle of huge fields of sunflowers. I felt so sad about all those families who'd worked hard on their little strips of land for years … and then had to sell to bigger farmers when they could no longer make a living.

We're not too far from Vichy. Marc hopes he'll be able to sell his pottery there – it gets quite a lot of tourists. And one day very soon, when we've settled in, I'll have to find a job myself – probably in Vichy. But what I'd really like to do is open a little village shop! (Shhhhhh.)

The house next door belonged to an old lady who lived alone. Her children had moved away years ago, to work in Paris. Now it's up for sale too, and we hear an English woman wants to buy it for a holiday cottage. There's a retired Swiss couple just down the road. We could get quite cosmopolitan!

▲ A view of Langy.

We met the new mayor of Langy yesterday. Young and lots of energy. He's determined to attract people back to live here, and especially younger people. He has been sending out posters inviting people to come and build here. We await the crowds.

Come down and see us soon. Fresh air, countryside, nightingales, cycling. And you know how Auvergne is famous for its extinct volcanoes. Vulcania – the volcano centre – is only an hour's drive away. You will really love it here.

Grosses bises

Jacqueline

▲ The church in Langy. It was built in the 11th century.

1 Langy is suffering from *rural depopulation*.
What does that term mean? (Look it up?)

2 Write down: **a** any causes **b** any consequences
of rural depopulation, given in Jacqueline's letter.
Give each as a full sentence.

3 This French road map shows the area around Langy.
(Langy is in H5, about 46° 16′ north of the equator.)
a Children from Langy now go up the N7 to primary
school in Varennes. How far is that, by the shortest
route? Measure to the centre of each settlement.
b When Jacqueline runs out of coffee she drives
down the N7 to a little shop in the middle of
St Gérand-le-Puy. About how far?

4 A craft centre at Boutiron, just north of Vichy, is keen
to sell Marc's pottery. It's at about 46° 9′ north.
Draw a sketch map of the roads, with road numbers,
telling Marc how to get there from Langy by car.
Add distances where you think that will help.

5 This table shows data for the whole Auvergne region:

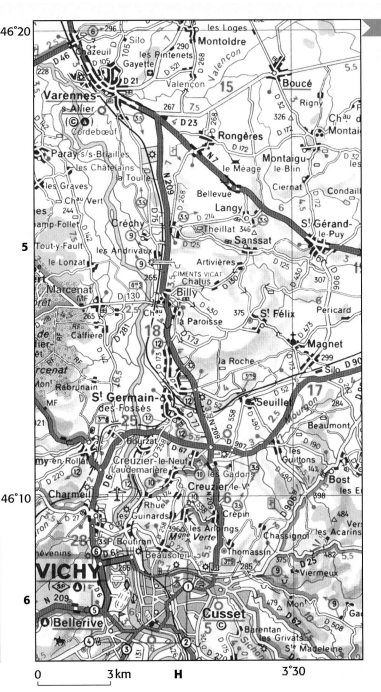

	1982	1990	2000
Population (millions)	1.33	1.32	1.31
Pop. density (people/sq km)	51.2	50.8	50.3
Natural increase in population (%)	− 0.01	− 0.06	− 0.12
Net migration	0.04	− 0.04	0.02
% of population aged 0–19	27.0	24.1	22.7
aged 60+	21.5	23.7	24.5
Life expectancy	74.6	76.7	78.2

a Auvergne had fewer people in 2000 than in 1982.
How many fewer? Give your answer as a full
number. (No decimal points!)
b The table shows *natural increase* and *net migration*.
Explain what each term means, and say what a
minus sign (−) shows. (Glossary?)
c In both 1982 and 2000, more people moved *into*
than *out of* Auvergne. But the population still kept
falling. Why?
d Overall, what is happening to:
  i the % of the population aged under 20?
  ii the % of the population aged 60 and over?
  iii life expectancy?
e If these trends continue, predict what the
population of Auvergne will be like in 2020.
f What effects might these trends have on the
region? Think of as many as you can.

6 This is the poster the mayor
sent out, offering people land
to build on in Langy. Cheap!
(About £2.10 per square
metre.)
a Do you think this offer
is likely to work?
Give reasons.
b Write a serious letter to
the mayor suggesting other
things he could do, to
attract people to live in
Langy. Think creatively!

VENEZ CONSTRUIRE A

LANGY

MOULINS

VARENNES S/A

N 209

D 214

N 7

ST GERMAIN DES F.- VICHY.

LAPALISSE - ROANNE.

• LOTS VIABILISES A €5 T.T.C LE M².
• IMPOTS LOCAUX TRES MODERES.
• JOLI BOURG AVEC EGLISE DU XI°S.
• EXCELLENTE SITUATION GEOGRAPHIQUE.

RENSEIGNEMENTS EN MAIRIE
TEL: 70.57.12.50
LUNDI 16h30 - 19h MARDI-VENDREDI 15h - 17h

The Paris problem

In this unit you'll look at another challenge that faced France: how Paris had grown overcrowded.

How Paris grew …

Paris is one of the world's most famous cities.

- It began on two little islands in the River Seine, now called the Île de la Cité (•) and the Île St Louis (○). Look for them on this map.

- A tribe was already settled on the islands, living by fishing, when Julius Caesar arrived and took control of France, over 2000 years ago.

- The settlement grew, spreading out in circles. By 1800, it had over half a million people.

- The graph below shows how it grew between 1900 and 2004.

- Today the ring road or **le Périphérique** (○) marks the boundary of the **City of Paris**.

- The City and built-up area around it from the **Paris conurbation**.

Why did it grow so large?

In France, everything has always been centred on Paris.

- It's the home of the government and big business. Most big French companies have offices there.

- There is a lot of industry in and around it.

- It's at the centre of the transport networks (road, rail, air travel) and the media (TV, radio, papers).

- It has a reputation as an exciting place to live.

Paris had far more power and influence than any other French city. It drew people from all over France, and from the countries France had colonised.

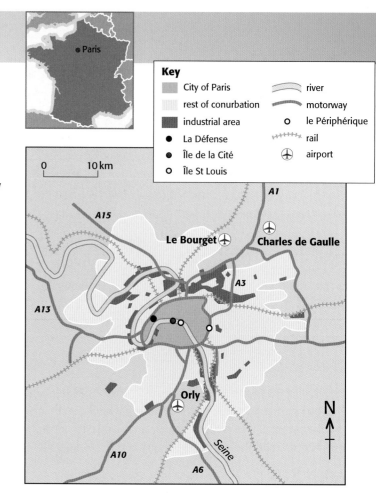

Key

	City of Paris	⌇⌇	river
	rest of conurbation	∿∿	motorway
	industrial area	○	le Périphérique
●	La Défense	⧓⧓	rail
●	Île de la Cité	✈	airport
○	Île St Louis		

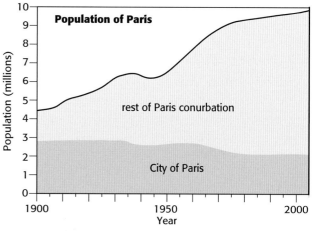
Population of Paris

▼ *It's Paris. Spot anything famous?*

The high life

A big population in a small area means a lot of high living!

In the City of Paris, most people rent apartments in blocks like these. (Even rich people.)

In the north and east of the City, many apartment blocks are run down and crowded.

The 1950s and '60s brought high-rise estates to Paris. Some became very run down.

But today, on the edges of Paris, modern estates are being built for well-off commuters.

The problems

By 1970 Paris had big problems. Terrible traffic jams, pollution, slums of run-down housing, much poverty, and not enough homes.

The problems were worst in the north and east, around the industrial areas. Look at the map on page 56.

How they tackled the problems

The government decided to:

◆ redevelop the suburbs at key points to give more (new) housing, offices, shops, and services such as health and sports centres. It chose La Défense, on the right, as one place to redevelop.

◆ build five brand new towns outside Paris, all within easy reach. You can find out more about these on the next page.

◆ get industries and other businesses to **decentralise** from Paris to other parts of France. This would help Paris *and* other regions.

▲ *Some of the modern buildings at La Défense.*

Your turn

1 What is a *conurbation*? (Glossary?)

2 Look at the graph showing the population of Paris.
   a What was the *total* population in 1900?
   b About how many times larger was it by 2000?
   c Between which years did it grow fastest?
   d What kinds of things would a city need to provide rapidly, to cope well with this kind of growth? (Jobs, health centres, …)
   You can give your answer as a spider map.
   e Paris could not provide these things rapidly, so the result was …?

3 Look at the steps taken to tackle the problem.
   a Which aimed to slow down the growth of Paris?
   b Which would improve life for people living there?

4 Draw a consequence map to show how decentralising business from Paris would help Paris *and* the regions. (See the start of a consequence map on page 43. The maps on pages 48 and 52 may help too.)

5 Look at the graph on page 56. After 1970, how did population change:
   a in the city of Paris?
   b in the rest of the conurbation?
   Suggest a reason for each. (For example, do you think the new towns became part of the conurbation?)

6 The population of the Paris conurbation is *still* growing. Write to the Prime Minister of France with your ideas for encouraging more people to move right out of the conurbation. (For example, to Auvergne?)

The new towns around Paris

Here you'll find out more about the new towns built outside Paris, with Marne-la-Vallée as our example.

Five new towns

By 1970 Paris was crowded, polluted, and packed with traffic. Something had to be done to take the pressure off. The answer? Five new towns.

This map shows the five towns, built around Paris. (Two are very close together.) The aim was to create:

◆ clean, green, pleasant environments to live in …

◆ … with good public transport into Paris, so that people could leave their cars at home …

◆ … but with plenty of local jobs, so that people did not *need* to commute into Paris.

Key

▨	City of Paris	═══	motorway
☐	rest of conurbation	⊢──⊣	railway (TGV)
▨	new town	⊕	airport
──	boundary of Île de France		

Marne-la-Vallée

One of the new towns is Marne-la-Vallée, built along the River Marne. It was developed around villages that already existed. Look at the map below, and all the photos.

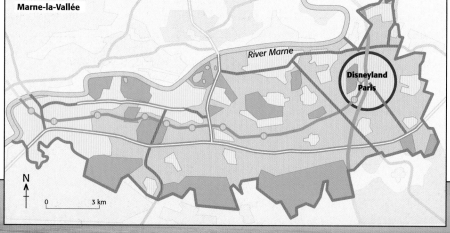

Key

	built-up areas
	woodland
	river, lakes
	open land
═══	motorway
▬▬▬	main roads
─○─	local railway to Paris, and stations
	TGV route (main French railway)

Marne-la-Vallée factfile

◆ 13 km from the centre of Paris

◆ 15 000 hectares

◆ 270 000 people by 2004

◆ over 2100 businesses by 2004

◆ over 118 000 jobs by 2004

Compare with Nottingham

◆ 7500 hectares

◆ 270 000 people by 2004

◀ *Marne-la-Vallée.*

▲ *Modern buildings in Marne-la-Vallée.*

▲ *It's a pleasant place to live …*

▲ *… and it has Disneyland Paris.*

Europe's Disneyland

Millions of people have visited Marne-la-Vallée already. (Including you ?)
Because it's the home of Disneyland Paris, which opened in 1992.
It gets around 12 million visitors a year.

Their population structures

Marne-la-Vallée	Age	City of Paris
	40+	
	20–39	
	0–19	

50 40 30 20 10 0   0 10 20 30 40 50
%   %

Your turn

1 The French government hoped the new towns would take the pressure off Paris. How might they do this? Think of as many ways as you can.

2 Look at the map showing the new towns.
Why do you think the government decided to:
a have five towns, instead of one very large one?
b arrange them in a circle like this?

3 Look at the motorways. They join the towns to Paris. Why was this a very important part of the plan?

4 Look at the map and aerial photo of Marne-la-Vallée.
a What differences do you notice between this town, and most towns in the UK?
b Compare the figures for Marne-la-Vallée, and Nottingham in the UK. What do you notice?

5 a Look at the table on the right, for the population of Marne-la-Vallée. Some numbers are in blue. Why?
b Draw a line graph for the data. Mark the *Year* axis up to 2020 and the *Population* axis up to 310 000.
c The town was planned with a maximum population of 307 000 in mind. Around which year will it reach that? How did you decide?
d How do you think they will stop the population going higher?

6 Compare the population structures, shown above.
a What differences do you notice?
b Come up with reasons to explain them.
c Name some services that might be in greater demand in Marne-la-Vallée than in the City of Paris.

7 They could have built Disneyland anywhere in France or the rest of Europe. Suggest reasons why:
a Marne-la-Vallée is a good choice
b the Marne-la-Vallée planners welcomed Disney.

8 You used to live in Paris, in the apartment block marked ◎ on page 57. But last month you moved to Marne-la-Vallée, to the house marked ● above. Write to your friend Alice (who lived next door in Paris) telling her your impressions of Marne-la-Vallée so far.

Year	Population of Marne-la-Vallée
1975	103 000
1982	152 000
1990	211 000
1999	246 000
2001	256 000
2010	291 000
?	307 000 (maximum)

France in the world

Here you'll find out why France has so much influence in the world, and learn about its interdependence with other countries.

France's political links

France has a great deal of political influence in the world. Once it was a colonial power. Now it's at the heart of the European Union.

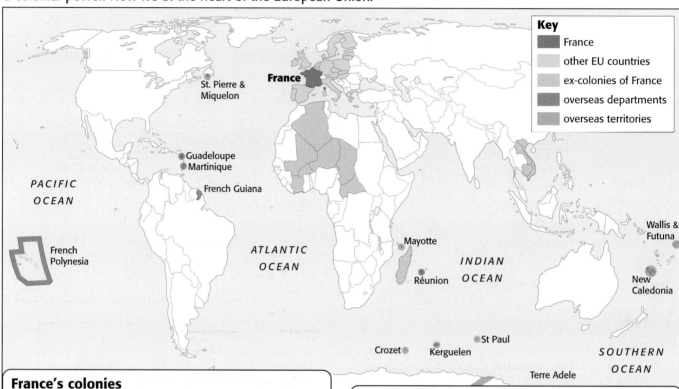

Key
- France
- other EU countries
- ex-colonies of France
- overseas departments
- overseas territories

France

St. Pierre & Miquelon

PACIFIC OCEAN

Guadeloupe
Martinique
French Guiana

French Polynesia

ATLANTIC OCEAN

Mayotte

INDIAN OCEAN

Réunion

Wallis & Futuna

New Caledonia

Crozet   Kerguelen   St Paul

Terre Adele

SOUTHERN OCEAN

France's colonies

France was the second largest colonial power after Britain. The map above shows colonies it held until they gained independence. In fact it had others too – but lost them in struggles with Britain and other nations.

- Some of the places it claimed remain as overseas **departments** and **territories**, and send politicians to the French Parliament.
- They give France a base in every ocean – which could be useful one day!
- They, and most of the ex-colonies, also do most of their trading with France.
- French is widely spoken in many of these places.

▲ *Many people from its ex-colonies have settled in France.*

France in the European Union (EU)

France and Germany were the key founders of the EU.
- Now the EU has 25 members, including the UK.
- The countries in the EU trade freely together, with no barriers. They also co-operate in many other ways.
- Today, the European Parliament is based in France, at Strasbourg in Alsace.

▲ *The home of the European Parliament in Strasbourg.*

Et aussi …

There are many other links too, between France and the rest of the world.

1 Culture

The world loves French culture.

◆ French cooking and wines find their way almost everywhere.
◆ Paris is one of the world's main fashion centres.
◆ French writers, philosophers, painters and film makers have influenced the world.

2 Trade

France trades heavily with other countries.

◆ It earned $358.5 billion from exports in 2003 – and spent $354.0 billion on imports.
◆ It trades all over the world, but mainly with other EU countries
◆ Outside the EU, its main trading partner is the USA. Inside the EU, it's Germany.

3 Tourism

France is the most visited country in the world!

◆ Over 70 million foreign tourists arrive in France each year …
◆ … and over 14 million French people go abroad as tourists.

4 TNCs

◆ There are many French transnational corporations (TNCs) with factories and offices all over the world.
◆ Examples are Renault and Peugeot (cars), Alcatel (electronics) and Michelin (car tyres and other things).

5 Treaties

France has signed many treaties with other countries. For example:

◆ to reduce global warming
◆ to protect the Antarctic
◆ against dumping of waste at sea
◆ against whaling.

6 Aid

◆ Like most MEDCs, France gives some aid to poorer countries.
◆ In 2002 it gave $5.4 billion in aid.
◆ Most of this went to its ex-colonies.

Your turn

1 The map on page 60 shows countries that were French colonies at the time they gained independence.
  a On which continent were most of these?
  b See if you can name the one from which France shipped tonnes of elephant tusks. (Page 129?)
  c Name four other ex-colonies of France.

2 Today France still has a base in every ocean. Try to think of ways this could benefit France.

3 Name six countries that France has close links with, through the EU.

4 The influence of France has spread to many countries. Try to give examples of ways it has influenced:
  a life in the UK
  b your life in particular.

5 a Draw a simple development compass rose (page 7).
  b At each point see if you can write two examples of links between France and other countries. For example what *natural features* link it to others?

6 Now write a short essay on *France's interdependence in the world.* (Glossary?) Not more than 250 words!

The big picture

This chapter is about **global fashion**, and **globalisation**. These are the big ideas behind the chapter:

◆ We are linked to real people all over the world, through the things we buy. Clothing is a good example.

◆ Most of the clothes we buy are made in other countries – and usually in poorer ones.

◆ Their manufacture is usually arranged by large companies from richer countries, who want to make as much profit as possible.

◆ The people who make the clothes you buy get only a very small fraction of what you pay for them, and some have to work in very poor conditions.

Your goals for this chapter

By the end of this chapter you should be able to answer these questions:

◆ What do these terms mean?
transnational corporation (or TNC)   globalisation   GDP
revenue   profit   sweatshop   exploitation

◆ In what ways does globalisation affect my life?

◆ Why do companies like to go global, if they can?

◆ Why are some TNCs more powerful than many countries?

◆ Why do companies like Nike and Quiksilver like to get things made in poorer countries, and in other people's factories?

◆ What kinds of conditions might you find in sweatshops?

◆ What is the role of the World Trade Organisation (WTO)?

◆ What are some benefits of globalisation? (Give at least three.)

◆ What are some disadvantages of globalisation? (Give at least three.)

And then …

When you finish the chapter, come back to this page and see if you have met your goals!

Country	Hourly wage in clothing factory ($)
USA	9.35
UK	9.50
Mexico	1.75
Malaysia	1.36
China	0.86
India	0.71
Sri Lanka	0.57
Indonesia	0.24
Pakistan	0.23

Did you know?
◆ Companies like Nike and Quiksilver don't really make clothes.
◆ They get companies in poorer countries to make them.

Did you know?
◆ China is the world's top exporter of clothing.

Did you know?
◆ The business of clothing humans is worth around 400 billion dollars a year.

Your chapter starter

Look at the clothes on page 62.

What do you think of them?

Who do you think made them?

Do you think they got paid much?

Why do clothes shops take a lot of trouble with their windows?

I don't think it's me.

Walter's global jeans

Here you'll see how an ordinary pair of jeans can involve many countries.

Cool or what?

Walter, trying on his latest birthday present. Not cool – but well-travelled!

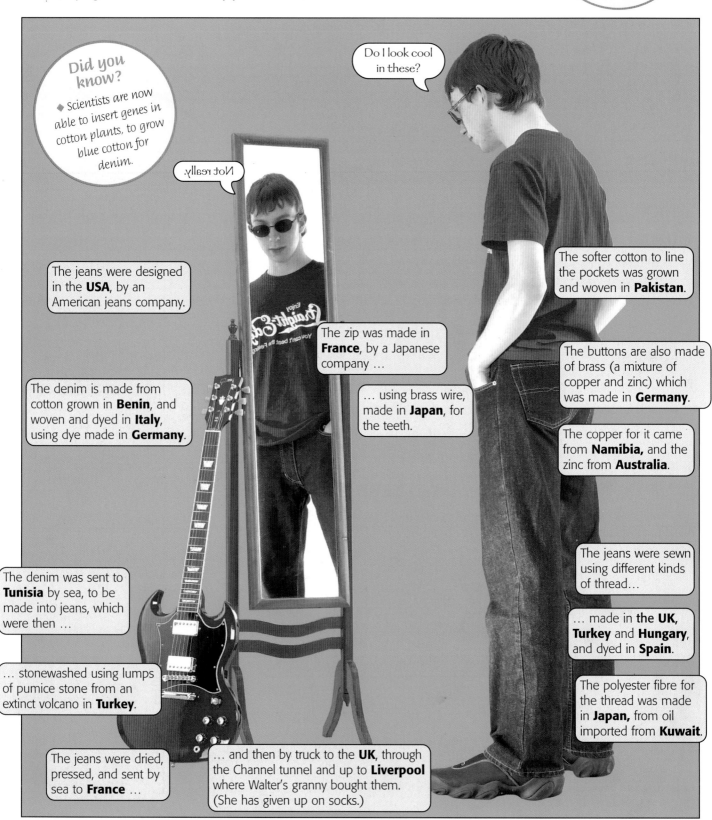

Did you know?
◆ Scientists are now able to insert genes in cotton plants, to grow blue cotton for denim.

Do I look cool in these?

Not really.

The jeans were designed in the **USA**, by an American jeans company.

The softer cotton to line the pockets was grown and woven in **Pakistan**.

The zip was made in **France**, by a Japanese company …

The buttons are also made of brass (a mixture of copper and zinc) which was made in **Germany**.

The denim is made from cotton grown in **Benin**, and woven and dyed in **Italy**, using dye made in **Germany**.

… using brass wire, made in **Japan**, for the teeth.

The copper for it came from **Namibia,** and the zinc from **Australia**.

The denim was sent to **Tunisia** by sea, to be made into jeans, which were then …

The jeans were sewn using different kinds of thread…

… stonewashed using lumps of pumice stone from an extinct volcano in **Turkey**.

… made in **the UK**, **Turkey** and **Hungary**, and dyed in **Spain**.

The polyester fibre for the thread was made in **Japan,** from oil imported from **Kuwait**.

The jeans were dried, pressed, and sent by sea to **France** …

… and then by truck to the **UK**, through the Channel tunnel and up to **Liverpool** where Walter's granny bought them. (She has given up on socks.)

Getting Walter's jeans together

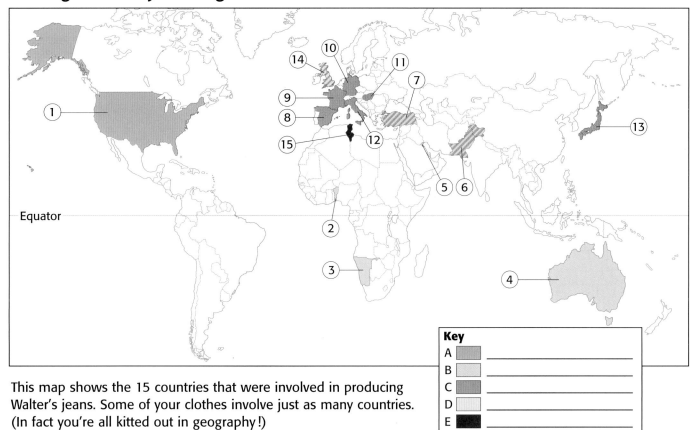

Key
A _____
B _____
C _____
D _____
E _____

This map shows the 15 countries that were involved in producing Walter's jeans. Some of your clothes involve just as many countries. (In fact you're all kitted out in geography!)

Your turn

1 Which *continents* contributed to Walter's jeans?

2 Name the countries marked 1 – 15 on the map above. Pages 128 – 129 will help. Answer like this: ① = ____
Then, after each country, write what it contributed to the jeans. (For example, *zip*.)

3 The map key is not complete. Complete it by matching the letters to the terms in italics below.
Give your answer like this: A = _____
manufacture and processing of materials
source of a raw material
making and finishing the jeans
design and brand name
country where jeans sold
The glossary may help, if you're stuck.

4 Some countries on the map (for example the UK) have stripes of a second colour. Explain why.

5 The table on the right shows wages in clothing factories. Use it and the map above to see if you can explain why:
a the American company didn't get the jeans made in the USA
b the denim was sent 1000 km from Italy to Tunisia, to be sewn into jeans.

Where your money goes when you buy a pair of jeans

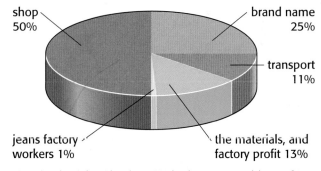

shop 50%
brand name 25%
transport 11%
jeans factory workers 1%
the materials, and factory profit 13%

6 a Look at the pie chart. Walter's granny paid £40 for the jeans for Walter. Of this, how much went to:
i the shop where she bought them?
ii the American company whose label they carry?
iii the worker(s) who sewed them?

b Does what you found in a seem fair to you? Explain.

7 Do you think Walter's jeans had any impact on the environment? Give reasons for your answer.

Hourly wages for clothing factory workers	
Country	**Average pay per hour (£)**
USA	6.64
UK	6.55
Italy	6.49
Tunisia	0.99

Behind the swoosh

the state of Oregon — USA

In this unit you'll see how Nike has spread around the world.

The Nike operation

Walter's jeans (page 64) were just ordinary. But what about labels like Nike?
Where are their clothes made?

Nike is based in Oregon in the USA. This is the headquarters from which the business is controlled.

The people who run Nike are anxious to make as much money as possible. So Nike keeps on …

… bringing out new designs for its clothing and trainers. But it does not *make* these things itself.

Instead it searches the world for places to get things made cheaply, in other people's factories.

Nike goods are made in nearly 40 different countries, mostly by young women like these.

While they are working really hard, so is Nike – getting people like you to buy things with the swoosh on.

Nike spends around a billion dollars in total on advertising, in around 140 different countries.

It pays top athletes millions to wear Nike products, as another way to advertise.

It supplies its goods to 47 000 shops round the world. (It owns just a fraction of these shops itself.)

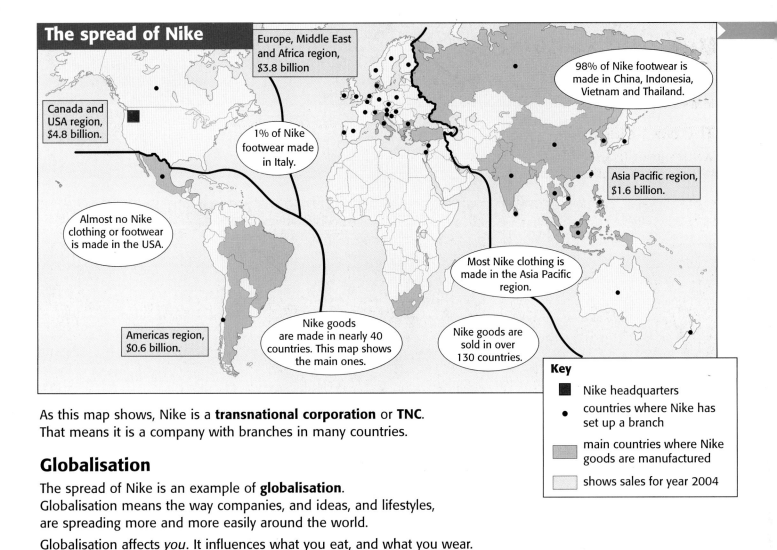

The spread of Nike

Europe, Middle East and Africa region, $3.8 billion

Canada and USA region, $4.8 billion.

98% of Nike footwear is made in China, Indonesia, Vietnam and Thailand.

1% of Nike footwear made in Italy.

Almost no Nike clothing or footwear is made in the USA.

Asia Pacific region, $1.6 billion.

Most Nike clothing is made in the Asia Pacific region.

Americas region, $0.6 billion.

Nike goods are made in nearly 40 countries. This map shows the main ones.

Nike goods are sold in over 130 countries.

Key
- ■ Nike headquarters
- • countries where Nike has set up a branch
- ▨ main countries where Nike goods are manufactured
- □ shows sales for year 2004

As this map shows, Nike is a **transnational corporation** or **TNC**. That means it is a company with branches in many countries.

Globalisation

The spread of Nike is an example of **globalisation**. Globalisation means the way companies, and ideas, and lifestyles, are spreading more and more easily around the world.

Globalisation affects *you*. It influences what you eat, and what you wear. When you decide what to buy, you affect people thousands of miles away.

Your turn

1 What kinds of goods does Nike sell? Write a list, and give prices if you can.

2 Using the map on pages 128 – 129 to help you, name:
   a six countries where Nike has a branch *and* gets goods made
   b two countries where Nike goods are made but Nike does not (yet) have a branch
   c eight other countries where Nike has a branch.

3 Nike is a *transnational corporation* or TNC. Its growth is an example of *globalisation*. Explain each of the two terms in italics.

4 Now compare the Nike map with the one on page 20.
   a Look at the GDP per capita for the countries where *most* Nike goods are made. What do you notice?
   b Suggest a reason why Nike chooses these countries.
   c On which *continent* does Nike *sell* most goods? Is it rich or poor?
   d Suggest a reason why Nike does not (yet) get goods made in countries like Ghana.

5 The spread of Nike is an example of globalisation. See if you can give at least *four* other examples. (Companies? TV programmes? Examples from sport or politics?)

6 Each of these helps the process of globalisation. For each, write a short paragraph to explain why.

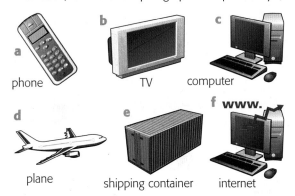

a phone   b TV   c computer
d plane   e shipping container   f www. internet

7 Now give six examples of how globalisation affects you. (Think about what you wear, and eat, and do in your free time.) Present your answer in an interesting way!

Why go global?

In this unit you will learn why companies like to spread around the world.

It's all about profit

Nike isn't alone. Thousands of companies have set up branches around the world to make things, or sell things, or both. So why do they go global? Because of this little equation:

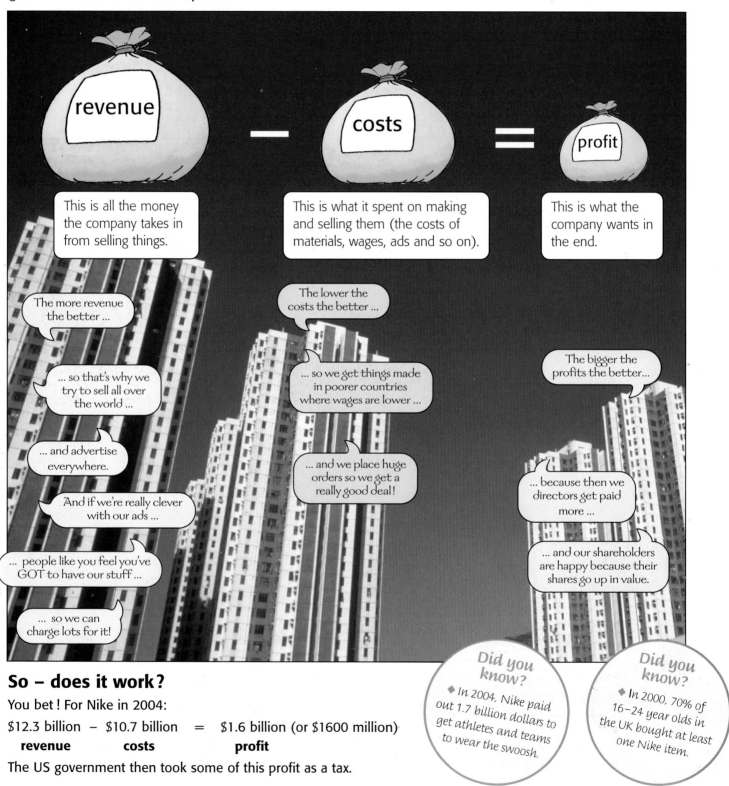

So – does it work?

You bet! For Nike in 2004:

$12.3 billion − $10.7 billion = $1.6 billion (or $1600 million)
revenue   **costs**   **profit**

The US government then took some of this profit as a tax.

Some other TNCs

Nike is very small compared with some TNCs, as this first table shows.
Wal-Mart, a supermarket chain, had over 20 times more revenue that year.

TNC	Its business	Based in	Revenue ($ billions)
Wal-Mart	supermarkets	USA	244
BP	oil/petrol	UK	233
Exxon Mobil	oil/petrol	USA	180
Toyota	cars	Japan	168
Nestlé	foods	Switzerland	49
Microsoft	software	USA	32
Coca-Cola	you know what	USA	21
McDonald's	you know what	USA	17
GAP	clothing	USA	15
Nike	sports goods	USA	11

Revenues for 10 TNCs (in 2000)

Country	GDP (or total wealth produced) ($ billions)
USA	10 980
India	3022
UK	1664
Belgium	298
Bangladesh	259
Switzerland	240
Nigeria	111
Tunisia	68
Ghana	44
Jamaica	10

GDP for 10 countries (in 2000)

Now look at the second table. It shows the GDP for ten countries for the same year. Many of the TNCs earned more than many of those countries !

In fact Wal-Mart's revenue beat GDP for over 180 of the world's countries. It even beat the *combined* GDP of 50 of the poorest countries !

Did you know?
♦ Wal-Mart owns Asda in the UK.

▶ Who gets over 47 million customers a day, in 119 countries ?

Your turn

1 Copy and complete, using terms from the brackets.
The more _____ a company sells and the _____ its _____ the higher its _____ will be.
(*money   profits   losses   costs   goods   lower*)

2 Like every company, Nike aims to increase its profits.
   a Make a *large* copy of the Venn diagram on the right. (Use a full page.)
   b On your diagram, write in **A–H** below, *in full*, in the correct loops. (Small neat writing!) If you think one belongs in both loops, write it where they overlap.
   A It gets 40% of its trainers made in China.
   B It runs a website.
   C It sponsors top school sports teams.
   D It closed its trainer factories in the USA.
   E It now owns no trainer or clothing factories.
   F It employs sports scientists.
   G It brings out new styles regularly.
   H It opened a branch office in Australia.

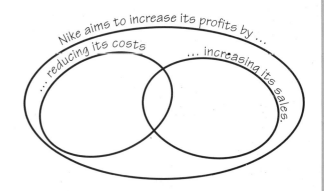

Nike aims to increase its profits by ...
... reducing its costs
... increasing its sales

3 Now look at the tables at the top of the page.
   a What is *GDP*? Give your answer as a sentence.
   b Make *one* list showing the 20 companies and countries, in order of revenue / GDP. (USA first.)
   c On your list, underline the countries in one colour and the companies in another. Add a key and a title.

4 Which do you think has more real power in the world, Wal-Mart or Ghana? Explain your answer.

A fashion victim?

Here you'll see how some of our clothes are made by exploiting people in poorer countries.

It's just the fashion

Nike is not the only company to get clothing made cheaply in poorer countries. Look at the list on the right. But who actually sews the clothes? It could be someone like Rosa in Manila.

Large % of clothing made in LEDCs *	
Calvin Klein	Levi Strauss
Ralph Lauren	Tommy Hilfiger
Quiksilver	Next
The Gap	Topshop
Principles	M & S
Warehouse	Miss Selfridge

* *This is <u>not</u> a complete list!*

Rosa's day

Rosa can hardly keep her eyes open. But she must must must concentrate. Otherwise she'll pierce her fingers. Or sew crookedly. If she does that, the supervisor will yell at her again.

She's tired because she worked overtime last night. Until 2 am. She didn't want to, but if you refuse they sack you on the spot. Everyone is forced to do overtime now for the big Christmas orders.

She dragged herself in again this morning, at 7 am. To sew non-stop, all day long, the side seams for sports joggers. Snatch a pair from the trolley beside you, slap them on the machine, race down each leg as fast as you can, throw them back on the trolley, grab another pair. On and on and on. By 8 her shoulders were aching. By 9 the heat was already stifling. And still an hour to go till the toilet break, when she can escape from the clatter of 500 machines for 10 minutes.

She thinks sadly about her family and village, like she does every morning. She left home just after her 16th birthday, 5 months ago. She was so excited about the job. They promised she'd earn enough to send some home. But the 280 pesos she gets (£4) for a 12-hour day is hardly enough to live on, when they take out rent and lunch.

Overtime again tonight. At 2 am she will leave the sewing section and drag herself past the guards, down the path by the barbed wire fence, to the room she shares with five others. Three bunk beds. No chairs. No wardrobe. She'll hang her clothes on the nails in the wall and climb into her bunk, too tired to talk to anyone.

More work tomorrow. It's usually six days a week, but in this busy period it's often seven. She wonders about the people who buy the clothes. If they could see her and her life, what would they think?

She wishes she could give up and go home. But she can't. She must earn, and there's no work in the village.

Adapted from newspaper articles, 2000

▲ *No rest for Rosa till she gets back …*
▼ *… to the hut that's now her home.*

Just one of many …

Over half the clothing in UK shops is sewn in LEDCs by girls like Rosa. Many are from rural areas, with little education.

Not all the clothes factories are bad. In fact some are more modern than UK factories. But there are many **sweatshops**, like Rosa's, where young women work in poor conditions, for very low pay. If the factory has no orders, they get no pay at all. They can be sacked without any notice.

How does it happen?

How does it happen that people like Rosa have to work in these conditions?
Again we take Nike as example – but it could be anyone:

1 Nice.

Off you go to find a factory then.

Nike designs a new range of clothing. Next, it has to be made!

2 Somewhere cheap ...

... that will do a good job and give no trouble ...

... but where we have a lot of control.

An executive goes to find a factory in an LEDC, where wages are low.

3 It's too low ...

... but if I say no, he'll go somewhere else.

Can't you do it for this much?

Okay.

The factory owner takes on the work – and aims to make a profit.

6 Mum, money. Please!

JUST IN

You're driving me mad.

The clothing gets finished on time. People like it. It sells really well.

5 We better just do it...

... since we don't have any choice.

The workers are not happy, but they need the jobs.

4 Just do it...

... or you're out. Okay?

So he forces his workers to work very quickly, for very little pay.

Shoppers have found out about sweatshops, and many have protested. Nike and other clothing companies now say they inspect all the factories they use, to make sure the workers are treated okay. But many thousands like Rosa are still being exploited – all in the name of fashion.

> **Did you know?**
> ◆ The head of Nike earns around 3000 times more per hour than Rosa does.

Your turn

1 Rosa usually works a 6-day week, 12 hours a day.
   a How much does she earn: **i** per hour? **ii** per week?
   b Does she get to keep all this pay?

2 Make a list of the working conditions in Rosa's factory. You can put them in order, with what you think is the worst thing first. (Is the low pay the worst thing?)

3 Now look at the chain above. What would happen if:
   a the factory owner refused to work for Nike's terms?
   b the factory owner increased his workers' pay?
   c the workers went on strike?
   d the customers didn't like the new clothing?
   e the government of the LEDC passed a law that factories there must pay higher wages?
   f customers refused to buy from Nike because of the sweatshops?
   g Nike forced the factories to pay their workers more?

4 Do *you* think Rosa is being exploited? (Glossary.) If so, who is exploiting her? Explain your answer.

5 Look again at the chain. Of all the people in it, who do you think:
   a has got *most* power to change things?
   b has got *least* power to change things?

6

The factories don't belong to Nike – so the workers are not their problem.

I like Nike things – so why should I care where they're made?

Write down what you will say to each person in reply.

7 **a** Draw a development compass rose (page 7) and give it the title *How globalisation has affected Rosa*.
   b Write in questions you could ask, to explore how globalisation has changed Rosa's life.
   c Under your questions, write in any answers you can. (Use a different colour.)

Global actions, local effects

Cardigan

In this unit you'll see how globalisation can lead to job losses too.

The other side of the story

On page 71 you saw how globalisation provides jobs for people like Rosa. Now let's look at the other side of the story.

Kelly's job takes flight

This is Kelly at her machine. Or rather, it was Kelly at her machine. But now the machine has gone, and Kelly is unemployed.

Kelly lives in Cardigan, in Wales. She used to work for Dewhirst, the UK clothing manufacturer, making jeans for Marks & Spencer. But now the factory has closed and Kelly has lost her job.

Why did the factory close ?

Most of Dewhirst's work was for Marks & Spencer. And that was the problem. Over the past few years, M & S had a difficult time, and its sales slumped. So Dewhirst's profits slumped too.

So Dewhirst decided it had to cut costs to survive. It still makes clothes for M & S – but overseas. It has set up factories in Morocco, Indonesia and Malaysia, where wages are much lower.

The Cardigan factory is not the only victim. Since 1998 Dewhirst has closed several of its UK factories, with the loss of around 2500 jobs.

Tears – and fears

'The managers called us in at the end of July', said Kelly. 'They told us the factory would close by November. We were shocked. Some women burst into tears. Some had been there for over twenty years ! We'd worked hard. But in the end that didn't matter. And now I'm afraid I won't find another job around here.'

Regret

'We regret having to close this factory', said a spokesman for Dewhirst. 'But sadly, it all comes down to pressure from shoppers. Shoppers want cheap clothes !'

Other jobs under threat too

In 1999, M & S sent out shock waves when it said it planned to get more clothes made overseas. For years it had tried to 'buy British', with over 70% of its clothing made in the UK. Now that figure is falling to 30% in an attempt to cut costs, and sell clothes more cheaply.

The UK clothing industry depended heavily on M & S. Kelly's job is not the first to go, and won't be the last.

(Adapted from news reports, November 2002)

▲ Kelly at her machine.

▲ One unhappy box, after Dewhirst announced its bad news.

▲ For over 100 years M & S had strongly supported the UK clothing industry.

Your turn

1 Why did Kelly lose her job? The flowchart below will explain. But first you need to do some work on it!

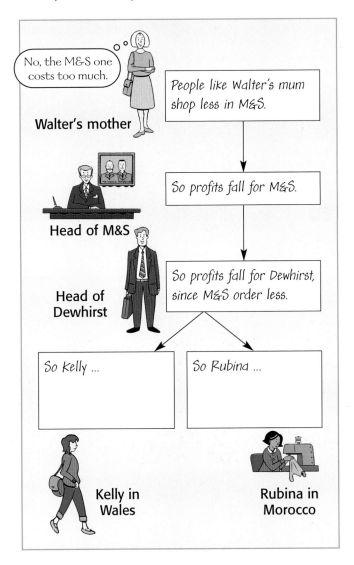

"No, the M&S one costs too much." — **Walter's mother**

People like Walter's mum shop less in M&S.

↓

So profits fall for M&S. — **Head of M&S**

↓

So profits fall for Dewhirst, since M&S order less. — **Head of Dewhirst**

↓

So Kelly ... — **Kelly in Wales**

So Rubina ... — **Rubina in Morocco**

a Make your own copy of the flowchart and drawings. (Just draw stick people.)
b Complete the sentences in the flowchart boxes.
c Walter's mother has a thought bubble. Draw bubbles for the others and fill them in, with thoughts about their part in the chain.

2 a Who will have gained, when Dewhirst moved production from Wales to Morocco? Think of as many groups as you can.
b Who may have lost out, when Dewhirst moved? (Was it *only* Kelly and the other factory workers?)
c Do you agree that Kelly was a victim of globalisation? Explain your answer.

Cut the workers' pay. / Charge M&S less. / Open the factory just three days a week. / Find new customers so that we don't depend on M&S. / DO NOT DISTURB

3 Above are some ideas a manager had, for saving the Dewhirst factory. Choose TWO of them. Say if you think they were good ideas, and give your reasons.

4 Textiles (cloth) and clothing were important industries in the UK for centuries. Now look at this graph:

People employed in manufacturing textiles and clothing, in the UK

a Is it true that the textile and clothing industries are *in decline* in the UK? (Glossary?) Give evidence.
b Try to give reasons for the trend the chart shows.

5

UK exports and imports of clothing ($ millions)					
Year	1990	1995	1998	2000	2002
Exports	3042	4648	4920	4111	3711
Imports	6961	8344	11 977	12 992	14 198

The table above shows exports and imports of clothing, for the UK (in millions of dollars).
a Show the export and import data, both on the same graph. (Use any suitable type of graph.)
b Describe any trends you notice.
c Give reasons to explain these trends.
d If these trends continue, predict what the clothing industry will be like in the UK by the year 2020.

6 Now think up ideas to save the UK clothing industry. (You can't prevent imports.) For example, could it focus on 'specialist' clothing? (Bullet proof? Heat proof? Luxury?) Think about help for young designers too. Put your ideas in a memo to the Prime Minister.

So is globalisation a good thing?

In this unit you'll look at arguments in favour of globalisation.

It's going on everywhere

There is globalisation in all kinds of business, not just clothing.
TNCs are spreading everywhere. Is this a good thing?

1 The TNCs think so. (They would!)

Well, we're the people who make globalisation happen.

We go where workers are cheap ...

... or markets are large ...

... and watch our profits grow!

2 Many governments in LEDCs think so.

And we need some TNCs (like oil companies), to help us exploit our resources.

We welcome TNCs ...

... because they give our people jobs ...

... and we hope the wages will help our economy.

3 Many governments in MEDCs think so.

We like to see our companies doing business overseas.

And we're happy when foreign TNCs set up here ...

It spreads our country's influence ...

... because it means jobs for people ...

...and either way, we collect taxes on the profits!

4 Many workers all over the world think so.

We've got jobs in TNCs. So we're lucky ...

But some of us have management jobs in our TNCs ...

... even if they're only sewing ...

... and don't pay much.

... and get good pay ...

... or at least it's good for here.

5 Many economists think so.

When TNCs open factories and branches in poorer countries ...

... it helps those countries to develop.

So of course we're in favour of TNCs.

Long live globalisation.

6 And the World Trade Organisation thinks so too.

If companies can move around freely ...

... and export and import freely ...

... it breaks down the barriers between nations ...

... AND it gives shoppers such a good choice!

So, many people are in favour of globalisation and think we all benefit.
But as you'll see in the next unit, many totally disagree!

More about the World Trade Organisation

The World Trade Organisation or **WTO** was formed to promote world trade. It is based in Geneva in Switzerland. Over 140 countries have joined it.

The WTO aims to remove barriers to trade between countries, so that companies can trade freely everywhere.

In the past, when countries fell out over trade they often went to war. The WTO aims to prevent this. For example, if Europe tries to stop a crop being imported from the USA, the WTO will try to settle the dispute peacefully.

Any country that joins the WTO must sign an agreement to obey its trade rules.

▶ *Everyone here yet? Getting ready for a WTO meeting.*

Your turn

1 For each of these people, write down what you think is the *main* argument in favour of globalisation:

the Manchester United football team

the president of McDonald's

the government of Vietnam, which lets TNCs get clothes sewn there, tax free

the president of Ghana, who has signed a deal with a UK mining company

Joe, unemployed in Glasgow, where a foreign TNC is about to set up a factory

Walter's mother, buying a new fridge in Liverpool

2 This is Priya. She is working in a call centre in Bangalore in India, for a British phone company.

Priya's job is to call and remind you, if you haven't paid your phone bill. She gets paid about £1800 a year. (The average wage in India is £300 a year.)

a Is this an example of globalisation? Explain.

b What do you think the phone company would say, in favour of globalisation?

c What do you think Priya would say, in favour of it?

d When it is 5 pm here it is 10.30 pm in Bangalore. What does that tell you about Priya's working hours?

3 The UK is a member of the WTO.

a What is the WTO? Give its full name in your answer.

b Write down two aims of the WTO.

c Write a short section for the WTO website saying why globalisation is a good thing. (120 words max.)

Against globalisation

In this unit you'll look at arguments against globalisation.

Does it do more harm than good ?

Lots of people are in favour of globalisation, and the spread of TNCs – and lots are against!

1   Many politicians around the world are against.

Some TNCs are far richer and more powerful than many governments ...

... so they just walk in and do what they want.

No one can control them!

And they move on the minute they find a better deal elsewhere.

2   So are some workers in LEDCs.

TNCs don't care about people ...

And most of the jobs they bring are badly paid ...

... only about profit.

... like sticking soles on these trainers.

They just use us for cheap labour.

So we're not learning skills that will help us in future.

3   So are some workers in MEDCs ...

Well, globalisation is why we lost our jobs.

Factories are moving to countries where wages are lower ...

... so we're left unemployed.

4   ... and many environmentalists everywhere.

Many LEDCs don't have strong laws to protect the environment ...

... so TNCs go there and ruin the place.

They pollute the air and water with toxic chemicals.

They wouldn't get away with it at home.

5   Some economists are not too happy either.

TNCs move most of their profits back home ...

... so they don't really help the countries where they have branches.

What LEDCs really need is their own industries.

But they don't have much chance to develop them ...

... with all this competition from TNCs.

6   Many people feel their culture is being eroded.

Baseball caps and jeans everywhere ...

... and fast food and fizzy drinks ...

... and TV shows that undermine our values.

So now our children think our culture is inferior.

Well I think you're cool, mom.

Protest goes global too ...

Many people are worried about the effect of globalisation on the world's poorer countries. They are especially worried about the World Trade Organisation, and its plans for free trade.

They say free trade just means TNCs are free to take over the world. And that it will help only the rich countries, and make poor countries poorer.

So protest has gone global too. When world leaders meet to discuss world trade these days, protesters from all over the world gather in their thousands.

... and can even get violent

In 2001 for example, the leaders of the G8 group of nations met to discuss world trade and other issues, at Genoa in Italy. Over 150 000 protesters turned up too. There were clashes between police and protesters. One protester was killed and 500 people injured.

(The G8 are the world's 7 richest industrial nations – the USA, Japan, France, Germany, Britain, Italy and Canada – plus Russia.)

Today, the G8 leaders tend to meet in isolated places, protected by thousands of police.

▲ *Get the message?*

Your turn

1 Page 76 shows things people say against globalisation. Using these to help you, write:
   a a *social* argument against globalisation
   b an *economic* argument against it
   c an *environmental* argument against it.
   Give each as a short paragraph.

2 Globalisation is a complex issue.
   a From pages 74 and 76, pick out two arguments that are *exactly* opposite.
   b Now see if you can find *at least two more* pairs of opposite arguments. Write them down.

3 The photo above was taken at a big protest meeting against the WTO.
   a Name three groups of people you might expect to find there. (Would directors of TNCs turn up?)
   b Study the message on the placard. Then rewrite it as a short speech. (Not more than 100 words.)

4 On the right is Naresh, a security guard in India. He's guarding a building 4000 km away, in California! The CCTV pictures are sent by satellite. If he sees a problem he can quickly raise the alarm.
   You live in India. Write a letter to an Indian paper, in favour of, or against, the way the Californian company is employing Indian people.

5 And finally, you have a really important job. You are one of the G8 leaders. (Decide for yourself which one.)
   a First, do you think it is possible to halt globalisation? Write a note to another G8 leader giving your views about this.
   b You *are* worried about the power of the big TNCs. Write a set of guidelines you want TNCs to follow when they set up in LEDCs. (You will discuss these with the other G8 leaders.)
   Your guidelines should have at least 5 points.
   Think of big issues. Pay? Profits? The environment?

The big picture

This chapter is about world trade in coffee and other crops. These are the big ideas behind the chapter:

◆ We are linked to real people all over the world, through the foods and drinks we buy. Coffee is one example.

◆ Millions of small farmers in LEDCs depend on crops such as coffee.

◆ The crops are usually bought by TNCs, which process and package them for sale in our shops.

◆ World prices of coffee and many other crops have fallen; this is helping to keep LEDCs poor, and TNCs in profit.

◆ Fair trade is a key way to help LEDCs escape poverty.

Your goals for this chapter

By the end of this chapter you should be able to answer these questions:

◆ What kind of climate does coffee need, and which coffee-growing countries can I name? (At least five!)

◆ Who gets the smallest share of the money from a cup of coffee?

◆ What has been happening to the world price of coffee beans, and why? And how is this affecting coffee farmers?

◆ How is Fairtrade coffee different from other coffees? And how does a Fairtrade company work with coffee farmers?

◆ Besides coffee, which other crops are suffering from falling prices? (At least five examples.) And why? And how does this affect LEDCs?

◆ What do these terms mean?
subsidy   *tariff*   *World Trade Organisation (WTO)*
fledgling industry   *G-20 group of countries*

◆ What example can I give of a trade rule that works against LEDCs?

◆ What is *free trade*? And why do many people think it's not fair trade?

◆ What kinds of things could help LEDCs earn more from trading? (Give at least three examples.)

And then …

When you finish the chapter, come back to this page and see if you have met your goals!

Did you know?
◆ Coffee is the world's most valuable traded commodity, after oil!

Did you know?
◆ The coffee industry is worth over $60 billion a year …
◆ … or about ten times Ghana's GDP.

Did you know?
◆ The first known coffee house in England opened in Oxford in 1650.

Did you know?
◆ In China people drink one cup of coffee a year, on average …
◆ … but coffee companies hope that will soon change.

Your chapter starter

Look at the photo on page 78. The cherries contain coffee beans.

What do you think the children are doing?

Why do you think they're doing it?

Who do you think will drink the coffee?

Can you name any countries where coffee is grown?

I haven't a bean.

Time for coffee

In this unit you'll learn how, and where, coffee is grown – and how the money you pay for a cup of coffee is shared.

Inside a cup of coffee

While you read this, millions of cups of coffee are being drunk all over the world. And hidden inside each one is months and months of toil.

When they get to their destination, the beans must be roasted before use. Some are then crushed and processed to give 'instant' coffee.

There the beans are checked for size and quality. Some are rejected. The rest are packed again, ready for export by ship.

The clean dry coffee beans are poured into 60 kilogram sacks. The sacks will then be brought to a coffee centre.

Coffee grows on trees. The coffee berries are called cherries.
They go from green to yellow to red as they ripen. In most places …

… the cherries are picked by hand. It's slow, because they ripen at different times! If it rains, the ripe ones get knocked to the ground.

Inside each cherry are two coffee beans. The beans are removed, washed well, then left to dry in the sun.

Your turn

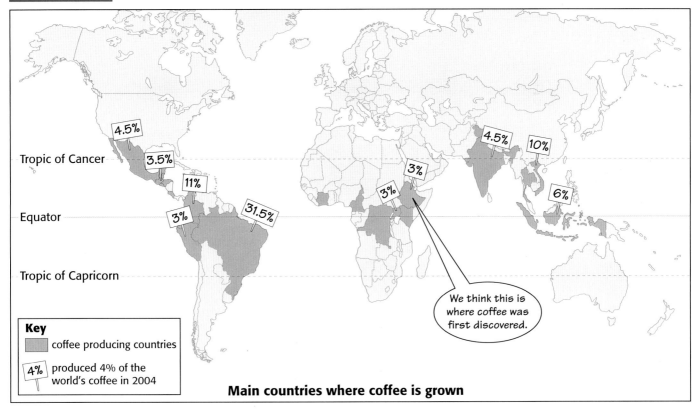

Main countries where coffee is grown

Key

coffee producing countries

4% produced 4% of the world's coffee in 2004

1 This map shows the main countries that grow coffee. It also gives the % share for the top 10 that year.
  a List the top 10 coffee growing countries and their % in order, the main one first. (Pages 128–129?)
  b Now draw a pictogram to show this data. (Think of a good way to show 1% of coffee.)
  c Add a final row to your pictogram to show the total share for the remaining countries. Label it.
  d Which *continent* comes top for growing coffee?

2 Write down each statement. Then if you think it's false, cross out the wrong part and correct it neatly.
  (Use what you know already. Page 80 will help too.)
  A Coffee is grown in the tropics.
  B Coffee trees need a cool climate.
  C Russia depends heavily on its coffee exports.
  D Dry weather is best for the coffee harvest.
  E The Philippines is a top coffee producer.
  F Ghana is the world's top coffee producer.
  G They think coffee was first discovered in Tunisia.
  H The coffee growing countries are all MEDCs.
  I The coffee you drink will have travelled by ocean.
  J The coffee industry is a global industry.

3 Look at the table on the right.
  a Are there any coffee growing countries in this list?
  b Are there any LEDCs in this list? (Page 20?)
  c What can you conclude from your answers for **a** and **b**? Give your answer as a full sentence.

4

shippers — growers — roasters/producers of final coffee

LEDC traders/exporters

5p 17p 30p 79p 44p

£1.75

café

This pie chart gives you an idea where the money goes, when you pay £1.75 for a coffee in a cafe.
  a What % does the grower get?
  b Who gets the largest share of the money?
  c Most of the money ends up in … ?
    i the LEDC that grew the coffee **ii** an MEDC
  d Where do you think most of the hard work is done?
    i in the LEDC that grew the coffee **ii** in an MEDC

Top 10 coffee-drinking countries, 2000			
Country	**kg/person**	**Country**	**kg/person**
1 Finland	9.88	**6** Netherlands	6.74
2 Norway	8.85	**7** Germany	6.73
3 Denmark	8.58	**8** Austria	5.46
4 Sweden	8.00	**9** France	5.44
5 Switzerland	6.95	**10** Italy	5.40

Bitter coffee

Here you'll find out why many coffee farmers can barely survive – even though more and more of us drink coffee.

Pedro Loria, coffee farmer

Most of the world's coffee is grown on small farms, by people like Pedro below. His farm is in Costa Rica, in Central America.

Growing coffee is hard work. Planting trees, watering in dry weather, spraying against disease, pruning, fertilizing, picking the cherries. But even when Pedro works really hard, it does not mean he'll earn more.

Because that's decided far away, in cities like New York and London, by people who'll never meet him. At a Commodity Exchange, buyers (mostly TNCs like Nestlé) buy up the coffee crops, often before the harvest.

And Pedro's problem is that, for several years now, he has earned very little. In spite of all his hard work, he has barely survived.

Another harvest over

It's the middle of February, and the coffee harvest has just finished. Pedro is worn out. For the last ten weeks he and his wife have been starting work at 5 am and picking coffee cherries all day.

This year he got paid a bit more for the beans. Not much more, but at least he can afford a school uniform for the oldest boy. The others are in hand-me-downs. He hasn't been able to buy them new exercise books or pens for months but he'll do that this week.

And at least the family hasn't starved. They grow vegetables, and keep chickens. Not like his neighbour's family, who had to go begging down on the road. Now the father has given up and gone to San José to look for work. His wife and children are struggling with the harvest.

It's a harsh world. Pedro hears from his cousin in London that you can pay a fortune for a coffee in a coffee bar. So why does he get so little for his beans? That makes him feel really bitter.

And what about next year? He does not know what he'll earn. But it could be far less than this year. Maybe, just maybe, it's time to give up.

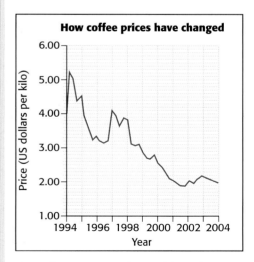

▲ Coffee prices on the world market dictate what Pedro earns.

Behind the coffee mystery

So why does Pedro get paid so little for his coffee beans?

It's because there's too much coffee grown! There are tonnes of beans in store around the world.

This is partly because the World Bank and other bodies have encouraged LEDCs to grow coffee.

So countries have competed to grow more and more, instead of agreeing a plan between them.

With so much coffee on the market, the buyers can push the price right down. They pay less …

… so the coffee farmers earn less. Less money for food, and clothes, and education for their children.

Meanwhile more of us like to drink coffee in smart coffee bars. So they can charge us more for it.

Your turn

1 Coffee beans are bought and sold in bulk at Commodity Exchanges, usually over the phone and internet. Who buys up most of the coffee crops?

2 Look at the graph on page 82.
 a What overall trend does the graph show?
 b What was the average world price for a kilo of coffee beans, at the start of: i 1998? ii 2003?
 c Give a reason for the big fall in price.

3 The diagram on the right shows the % change in prices and profits for coffee, over a three-year period. (The figures for 1998 are taken as 100%.)
 a From 1998 to 2000, by what % did:
  i the world price of coffee beans fall?
  ii the price of instant coffee in the shops fall?
 b Now look at the company's profits. How did they change over the same period?
 c Suggest a reason for the change in b.

4 When too much coffee is grown:
 a who are the winners?   b who are the losers?

5 The price of coffee on the world market can rise as well as fall, from year to year. Say how each of these might affect it.
 a The coffee growing countries produce bumper crops.
 b A disease destroys all the stores of coffee beans.
 c A freak frost in Brazil kills all its coffee trees.
 d Coffee-drinking gets really popular in China.

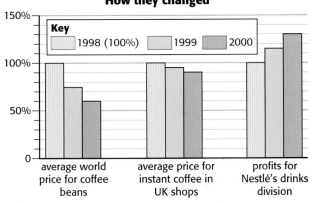

How they changed

83

A fair price for coffee farmers

This unit looks at what can be done to help the coffee farmers earn a fair price for their coffee.

How the world market works

On the world market, the price of coffee depends on just two things:

◆ the **supply** of coffee – how much is for sale
◆ the **demand** for it – how much people are prepared to buy.

And while the trading goes on, no-one thinks at all about the coffee farmers, or how much they need to earn to survive.

Another way to look at it

In 1986, a group of people in the Netherlands came up with a new way to buy and sell coffee, that keeps the farmers in mind:

Decide on a fair price to pay the farmers.

They called it **fair trade**, and created the **Fairtrade** logo.

In 1992 Oxfam and other British charities took up the idea, and started the **Fairtrade Foundation** to promote fair trade.

Fairtrade coffee

This is how fair trade works for coffee:

> A coffee company and a group of coffee farmers decide to work together.

⬇

> They agree a price for the coffee, that covers the cost of growing it and the farmers' cost of living – plus some extra.

⬇

> The company pays some of the money in advance, before the harvest, so that the farmers won't run short.

⬇

> The Fairtrade Foundation has to check the deal, before the company can use the Fairtrade logo on its coffee.

⬇

> In the shops, people who want to help the coffee farmers will buy the coffee – and they don't mind that it costs a bit more.

In return the coffee farmers promise to treat *their* workers fairly, and look after the environment – and to use the extra money for development projects in their area.

How is it going ?

Sales of Fairtrade coffee are rising fast in the UK. And not just coffee. You will see the Fairtrade logo on tea, sugar, fruit, juices, chocolate, honey, roses, wine – and even footballs ! And more goods are on the way.

And it's not just in the UK. Fairtrade goods are now sold in 19 countries.

▲ *Many coffee farmers around the world can barely make a living.*

▲ *It's not Fairtrade if it doesn't have the logo.*

▲ *Fairtrade is not just for coffee …*

How Fairtrade helps the coffee farmers

The Fairtrade movement helps many thousands of coffee farmers.

Miguel is one. He lives in a remote part of north east Costa Rica. He and a group of other coffee farmers sell their coffee beans to a British Fairtrade coffee company.

'Fairtrade has saved us' said Miguel. 'It means we can go on growing coffee. But that's not all. We used the extra money to get electricity and drinking water laid on for our community. And we've set up a scholarship fund to help students go to secondary schools, and even university.'

'You see, fair trade is all the help we need. We don't need charity!'

> **Did you know?**
> ◆ Costa Rica has a high adult literacy rate: 96%.
> ◆ Its first president was a teacher and knew education was very important.

But what about all the other coffee farmers ?

Fairtrade can help only a fraction of the small coffee farmers. Many millions more are at the mercy of the world trading system. Oxfam and other groups made suggestions to help these too:

A Get the coffee growing countries to DESTROY some of their STOCKS OF COFFEE BEANS. (The poorest beans.)

B Get the coffee TNCs to PAY EXTRA TAX on their big profits – and give the money to the COFFEE GROWERS.

C The coffee growing countries should AGREE WITH EACH OTHER how much to grow each year – and STICK TO IT.

D Help the coffee growing countries to make INSTANT COFFEE for export.

You'll explore these suggestions in 'Your turn.'

▲ It's still hard work. But now this Fairtrade coffee farmer is getting better paid.

Your turn

1

shopper → supermarket manager → from Fairtrade company → coffee farmer

The people in this chain are linked by fair trade.

a Make a large copy of the chain. Give each person a speech bubble, big enough to write a sentence in.

b Write each of these in the correct bubble – and then complete the sentence:
By buying coffee beans directly, we …
Now I can get on with growing coffee, without …
I like to buy coffee that …
We make a fair profit on the coffee – so …

2 Look at your drawing for **1**.

a Is there a loser in the chain? If so, who?

b Is there a winner in the chain? If so, who?

3 Look at how Fairtrade companies work with coffee farmers. Do you think it's *sustainable*? Explain.

4 Now look at suggestions Ⓐ – Ⓓ above.

a Ⓐ might seem a bit shocking. See if you can explain how it would help coffee growers.

b Which other suggestion could reduce *supply*?

c Which do you think would be fastest to carry out?

d Which might take longest? (At least a few years.)

e Which might be the most difficult to carry out? Why?

f Explain how Ⓓ would help coffee growing countries. (Check the pie chart on page 81?)

g Now draw a consequence map like the one begun here, for Ⓓ. Add as many boxes as you can.

5 It's time to choose ! You could put money in a collection box to help coffee farmers, or buy Fairtrade coffee. Which do *you* think the farmers would prefer? Explain.

> Coffee growers make and export instant coffee …
> ↓ which means
> … they earn more money …
> ↓ so

The wider picture

Here you'll see how world trade very often works against LEDCs – and look at some suggestions for solving the problem.

It's not just coffee

You saw earlier how the price of coffee has fallen over the years. But it's not just coffee. Look at the table on the right. Disaster !

The main reason for the fall in prices of these crops is that too much is grown. And that's because:

◆ more countries have started to grow them
◆ fertilizers and pesticides and better seeds lead to bigger harvests.

So who are the winners and losers ?

◆ The main losers are the farmers in LEDCs who depend on these crops. They get poorer and poorer.
◆ The main winners are the big TNCs that process the crops into the goods we buy in the shops. The bigger the supply the more cheaply they can buy – so the bigger their profits. (See page 68.)

% fall in real prices for crops 1980–2000	
bananas	- 4%
tea	- 8%
soybean	- 39%
maize	- 42%
wheat	- 45%
cotton	- 48%
palm oil	- 56%
rice	- 61%
coffee	- 65%
cocoa	- 71%
sugar	- 77%

And trade rules don't help !

Some of the crops (like sugar) are grown in MEDCs too. But there, many farmers get **subsidies** to grow them.

Then the MEDCs export the crops around the world, in competition with the LEDCs. The LEDCs can't really win, even at home !

But if the LEDCs try to export those crops to MEDCs that grow them, they come up against **tariffs** (taxes) that put buyers off.

Now think about cocoa. Ghana and other countries sell it to TNCs, who ship it to MEDCs and turn it into chocolate and other goodies.

They export these all around the world, and make lots of profit from them. Nice for the MEDCs – who don't even grow the cocoa !

But if Ghana and other cocoa growers make chocolate, and try to export it to the MEDCs, they find … those tariffs again !

Is free trade the answer?

The World Trade Organisation or WTO makes the rules on world trade. The WTO is made up of members from 146 countries, rich and poor. The rich countries are in favour of **free trade**. That means:

◆ Countries could export crops and other goods, and even services, freely to any country. All tariffs would be dropped.

◆ TNCs could set up anywhere, and governments could not refuse them.

But many people fear this will help the rich countries and TNCs much more than the poor countries. They think free trade is *not* fair trade.

Other approaches

Many people think the WTO and rich countries must do far more to help LEDCs escape from poverty, through trade. Here are some of their ideas:

Ⓐ Get the LEDCs to agree on how much of a crop to grow, to control the supply. And help them switch to other crops if necessary.

Ⓑ Force TNCs to pay a decent price for the crops they buy – not just the lowest price they can get away with.

Ⓒ Help poorer countries to process their own crops into foods for sale.

Ⓓ Remove all tariffs in MEDCs for crops and foods from LEDCs.

Ⓔ Allow LEDCs to use tariffs to protect their own fledgling industries, until they get strong enough to compete.

Ⓕ Poorer countries must have the right to keep TNCs out if they wish, to protect their own growing companies.

A fairer future?

In the past, the rich countries have had most power in the WTO. But now 20 LEDCs, including China, Brazil and India, have formed the **G-20 group**, to make sure the poorer countries get heard.

World leaders have set a goal to halve world poverty by 2015 (page 32). Many people think that trade, not aid, is the best way to make this happen. So they hope the WTO will soon help to make trade more fair.

▲ *Ms Dynamite sings out for fair trade.*

Did you know?
Sugar is obtained from ...
◆ sugar cane, grown in tropical countries, and...
◆ sugar beet, grown in cooler countries like the UK.

Your turn

1 We are all linked to people all over the world. How many foods from the table on page 86 do you eat or drink, linking you to farmers in LEDCs?

2 a Draw a bar graph to compare the price falls for different crops, given in the table on page 86.
   b The TNCs benefit when crop prices fall. Explain why.
   c Do they benefit at the farmers' expense? Explain.
   d Do you think you benefit too? Explain.

3 A fall in crop prices holds back development in LEDCs. Explain why. Give your answer in any form you wish. For example as a flowchart, a strip of drawings like those in this unit, a newspaper report, or a speech by Ghana's Minister of Trade, to the WTO.

4 Explain what these terms (from this unit) mean:
   subsidy   tariff   fledgling industry   the G-20 group

5 If there were free trade:
   a countries could export crops freely, without tariffs. How could this: i help LEDCs? ii harm them?
   b TNCs could open factories anywhere they chose. How could this: i help LEDCs? ii harm them?

6 Now look at each of the suggestions Ⓐ–Ⓕ above.
   a For each say briefly how it would help an LEDC.
   b You are Pedro from page 82. Put Ⓐ–Ⓕ in order of priority from your point of view, most urgent first.

7 Overall, are Ⓐ–Ⓕ tilted in favour of LEDCs, or of MEDCs? Do you think this is fair? Give reasons.

The big picture

This chapter is about how we can look after our planet. These are the big ideas behind the chapter:

◆ Our local actions may have global effects – for better or for worse.

◆ We have already done a lot of damage to our planet, through our local actions.

◆ Now we must take local action to protect it.

◆ Protecting it needs planning, and managing, and for all of us to work together.

Your goals for this chapter

By the end of this chapter you should be able to answer these questions:

◆ What does the slogan 'Local actions, global effects' mean, and what examples can I give?

◆ Where does the River Rhine rise, and which countries does it flow through, and where does it end up?

◆ What kinds of things is the Rhine used for? (At least five examples.)

◆ By around 1950 the Rhine was in a ruined state. Why?

◆ What is being done to help the Rhine recover?

◆ Which are Britain's National Parks, and why were they set up?

◆ What kinds of conflict can arise in a National Park?

◆ Who manages our National Parks, and what kinds of things do they do?

◆ Where is Antarctica, and what geographical facts can I give about it? (At least five.)

◆ In what ways has Antarctica been under threat in the past?

◆ What is being done now, to protect Antarctica?

◆ What kind of work goes on in Antarctica?

◆ What do the protection of the Rhine, the Peak District and Antarctica have in common?

And then …

When you finish the chapter, come back to this page and see if you have met your goals!

Did you know?
◆ The UK used to ship tonnes of rubbish out to sea, to dump it …
◆ … but now most dumping at sea is illegal.

Did you know?
◆ A banana skin dropped in Antarctica would take 100 years to break down.

Did you know?
◆ Chemicals you put down the sink can harm fish in the ocean …
◆ … even if you live miles from the coast.

Did you know?
◆ Many people think that climate change is the biggest challenge facing the human race.

Your chapter starter

Look at the photo on page 88.

What's going on here?

What's climate change?

What has it got to do with 'Local actions, global effects'?

What has it got to do with you?

Phew, it's hot in here!

How to ruin a planet

Here you'll learn how we are ruining planet Earth – and how we must protect it.

Get ready to ruin

So how do you ruin a planet? You can do it very quietly, little by little, place by place, year by year, like this.

Take a clean stretch of river

Take a clean, sparkling stretch of river, full of fish and other river life.

Dump harmful waste from factories and farms into it …

… and half-cleaned-up sewage from homes, and old tins and bottles …

… and lots of other rubbish, and you could end up with this. Yippee!

Take some fresh air

Take some clean fresh air, rinsed by the rain, that feels just great to breathe.

Add tonnes of waste gases, and dust, from factories and mines …

… and fumes from cars, power stations, factories, homes. Add sprays …

… of all kinds from everywhere. The result: air like this. Genius!

Take some fine land

Take some fine land with healthy soil, and lots of trees and wildlife.

Cut down the trees. Drive out the wildlife. Ruin the soil with crop after crop.

Pack it with fertilizers and other chemicals. Or dig it up looking for minerals.

Or use it as a rubbish dump. And you could achieve this. Well done!

It all adds up

We can all help to ruin the planet. Just do a few little things every week. Our small local actions will have a global effect. For example:

◆ The more electricity we can waste, the more fossil fuel gets burned – so we can bring on **global warming** even faster. And that will affect living things everywhere.

◆ The more chemicals we can pour down our sinks, the more harm we can do to our rivers. They will carry the chemicals all the way to the ocean. Great ! We can even harm polar bears that way.

But the good news is ...

The good news is: we humans are not really stupid. We can see that we are harming our planet. And that when we harm it, we harm ourselves. So we are learning some important lessons:

▲ Chemicals called PCBs, that we use in inks, paints and plastics, have been found far away, in polar bears.

If we don't start to live in a more **sustainable** way, we'll wreck our planet.

Each of us can help to protect the planet (just as each of us can harm it).

To protect places, we must **plan** and **manage** and **work together**.

Our local actions will give a global result: a better Earth for our children.

In the rest of this chapter

This chapter has three case studies to show you those lessons in action:

◆ along the **River Rhine** in Europe

◆ in the **Peak District National Park** in the UK

◆ on the continent of **Antarctica**.

You will learn about problems and conflicts in these places, and what we are doing to protect them.

Your turn

1 Three different types of pollution are shown on page 90: of water, air and land.
   a What does *pollution* mean ? (Glossary ?)
   b Put them in order, starting with the one you think has the biggest global effect. How did you choose ?

2 Whose *fault* do you think it is, that we damage our planet ? Is it anyone's ? Explain your answer.

3 a What does *Local actions, global effects* mean ?
   b Give an example of a local action with:
      i a 'good' global effect ii a 'bad' global effect.

4 Look at card **1** above.
   a What does *sustainable* mean ?
   b Give 3 things *you* could do to live more sustainably.

5 What will this planet be like 100 years from now, if we don't take care of it ? You are a time traveller. Write a letter to yourself, from 100 years in the future, describing the state of the planet.

6 You are a protector of the planet.
   a Design a T-shirt to remind yourself of your role.
   b Make up a slogan to describe your role.

Case study 1: The Rhine

In this unit you'll learn where the River Rhine is, and about the many demands that are made on it.

Meet the River Rhine

The Rhine is Europe's busiest river. This map shows its route from its source in the Alps to its mouth in the North Sea. Look how many countries it flows through, and how many more edge into its **drainage basin**.

Rhine factfile

◆ It is 1320 km long.

◆ Its drainage basin has an area of 185 000 km².

◆ About 55 million people live in its drainage basin.

◆ It provides water for 20 million people.

◆ It flows through one of the most densely industrialised regions in the world.

You will need to look at both maps in this unit to help you answer these questions.

Your turn

1 *glacier source delta mouth drainage basin*
   These terms are used in this unit. See if you can explain what each one means.

2 Draw a large sketch map of the Rhine. (Use a full page.) On your sketch map mark in:
   a the countries and main cities it flows through
   b the Alps   c other mountainous areas
   d Lake Constance   e the North Sea
   f industrial areas g agricultural areas
   h the names of the different sections of the river.

3 Each section of the Rhine has its own name. Which section:
   a has most industry around it?
   b do you think has most agriculture along it?
   c do you think has most people living around it?
   d has the narrowest, steepest, rockiest river valley? Explain your choice.
   e has the coldest water? Explain your choice.
   f has most sediment deposited? Give reasons.
   g has least sediment deposited? Give reasons.
   h has most hydroelectricity stations? Why do you think that is?
   i has most water running through it?
   j is on the flattest land? Explain your choice.

4 The Rhine is used for many different purposes.
   a Make a conflict grid like the one started below, and extend it to show two more uses of the Rhine. Complete all the labelling.
   b Now put ✔ where you think two uses are in harmony, ✘ where they conflict with each other, and o where they have no effect on each other.
   c Overall, would you say the level of conflicting demands on the Rhine is high, or low?

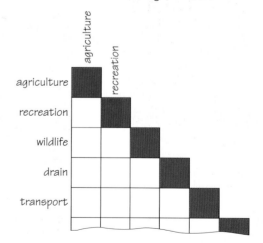

5 You are in charge of the Rhine. Pick out two conflicting demands on it, and say how you would resolve them.

A hard-working river

Many demands are made on the Rhine …

9 It's a home to wildlife. 200 years ago it was famous for salmon.

10 It's a link between inland Europe and the rest of the world. (Rotterdam is the largest port in the world.)

North Sea
Rotterdam
Rhine Delta
Lobith
Lower Rhine

0   100 km

7 It's like a motorway ! Hundreds of ships and barges sail up and down it every day, carrying cargo. Ships can go up as far as Basel.

Duisburg
Dusseldorf
Cologne
Bonn
Middle Rhine
B
Mainz
Bingen

8 It's a recreation centre. Tourists take cruises on it. Local people sail on it and relax on its banks.

Mannheim

6 It acts as a drain – for sewage and other waste from homes and factories.

N

5 It provides water for hundreds of factories – mostly for keeping pipes and tanks cool. The water is drained back into the river.

Upper Rhine

Strasbourg

Lake Constance

High Rhine

Basel
A

Alpine Rhine

4 It provides water for homes – for drinking, cooking and washing. (The water is cleaned up first.)

3 It is used for **irrigation** (watering crops). 10% of its water is taken for this, mainly in Holland.

ALPS

1 The Rhine rises in the Alps, fed by water from rain and glaciers. It runs into Lake Constance which acts as a huge reservoir.

2 From early in its journey, the Rhine is used to give hydroelectricity. Many of the reservoirs behind the dams are used for water sports.

Key

~ rivers

▨ industrial areas

☐ agriculture (crops, pasture, vineyards)

▨ forest

⩕ mountains

○ hydroelectricity stations

◉ cities and towns (not all shown)

● **A, B** needed for question 1 on page 97

╱ end of named section of the river

In this unit you'll learn how the Rhine was ruined by humans.

Poisoned by pollution

People living along the Rhine have always dumped their waste in it. But until 1800 there were not many people, and most of the waste was **biodegradable** – it could be broken down by bacteria.

Then the Industrial Revolution came to the Rhine basin. Mines were dug. Factories were opened. Towns and cities grew fast. As the years passed, more and more stuff ended up in the river, and much more of it was harmful.

▲ *On its way to the river. Nice ...*

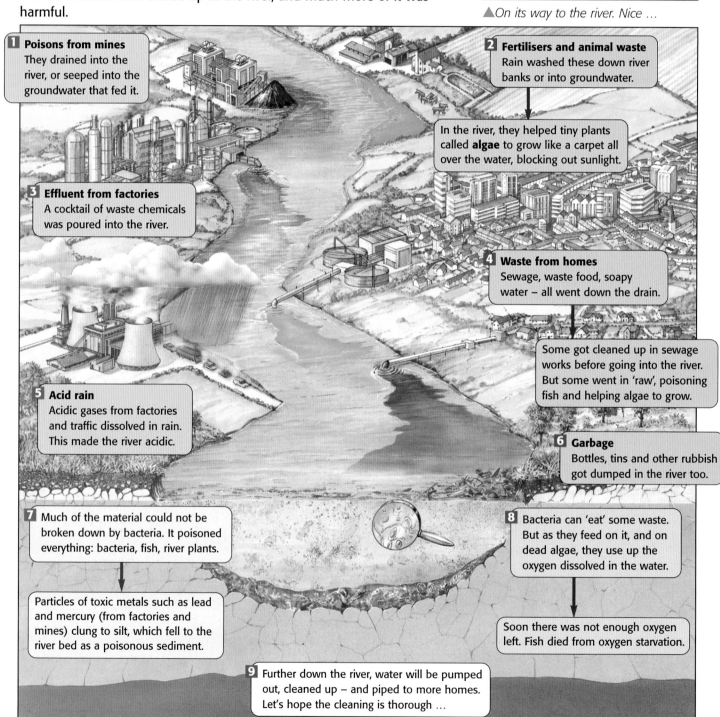

1 Poisons from mines
They drained into the river, or seeped into the groundwater that fed it.

2 Fertilisers and animal waste
Rain washed these down river banks or into groundwater.

In the river, they helped tiny plants called **algae** to grow like a carpet all over the water, blocking out sunlight.

3 Effluent from factories
A cocktail of waste chemicals was poured into the river.

4 Waste from homes
Sewage, waste food, soapy water – all went down the drain.

Some got cleaned up in sewage works before going into the river. But some went in 'raw', poisoning fish and helping algae to grow.

5 Acid rain
Acidic gases from factories and traffic dissolved in rain. This made the river acidic.

6 Garbage
Bottles, tins and other rubbish got dumped in the river too.

7 Much of the material could not be broken down by bacteria. It poisoned everything: bacteria, fish, river plants.

Particles of toxic metals such as lead and mercury (from factories and mines) clung to silt, which fell to the river bed as a poisonous sediment.

8 Bacteria can 'eat' some waste. But as they feed on it, and on dead algae, they use up the oxygen dissolved in the water.

Soon there was not enough oxygen left. Fish died from oxygen starvation.

9 Further down the river, water will be pumped out, cleaned up – and piped to more homes. Let's hope the cleaning is thorough ...

Mangled by man

Meanwhile, people also dammed and banked and straightened the river, to make it behave as they wished. Work was carried out at over 450 places along the river – mostly to help ships sail up it easily.

At the same time, the Rhine basin was being developed fast.

Each country did its own projects without worrying about the rest of the Rhine. The result was … more problems.

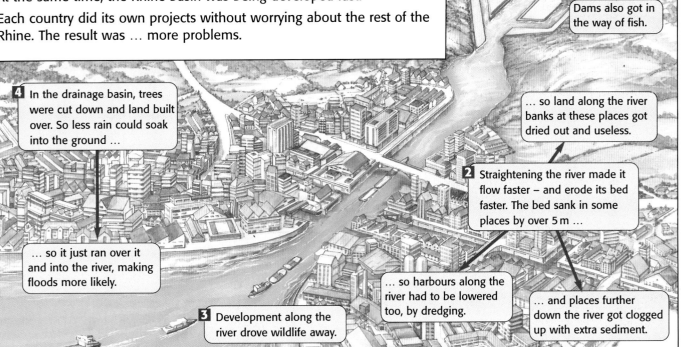

1 Dams caused erosion to speed up in some places further down the river.

Dams also got in the way of fish.

4 In the drainage basin, trees were cut down and land built over. So less rain could soak into the ground …

… so land along the river banks at these places got dried out and useless.

2 Straightening the river made it flow faster – and erode its bed faster. The bed sank in some places by over 5 m …

… so it just ran over it and into the river, making floods more likely.

… so harbours along the river had to be lowered too, by dredging.

… and places further down the river got clogged up with extra sediment.

3 Development along the river drove wildlife away.

Your turn

1 What do these terms mean?
biodegradable   effluent   bacteria
Industrial Revolution   groundwater
Give each answer as a full sentence.

2 Pollution in the Rhine grew steadily worse from around 1850 onwards. Suggest reasons.

3 By 1960 the Rhine was smelly and disgusting.
a Make two lists side by side, as started here:

Pollution of the Rhine	
CAUSES	CONSEQUENCES
factory effluent	

b Do each list on its own. (You should not try to match them up at this stage.) Do you think you should give *spoiled the look of the river* and *made the river smelly* as consequences?

c Now draw arrows linking each cause to *all* its consequences. (Your arrows will criss-cross.)

4 The Rhine used to be famous for salmon. By 1960 they had gone. Look at the panel on the right. Then explain what part:
a pollution   b engineering works
may have played in their disappearance.

5 Give three examples of how local actions in one Rhine country had unwanted effects in others.

6 Could pollution in the Rhine affect:
a the North Sea?   b you?
Give reasons for your answers.

7 It's 1960. The Rhine is a mess. You are the leader of the Netherlands. Write to the leaders of the other Rhine countries with ideas for saving the river.

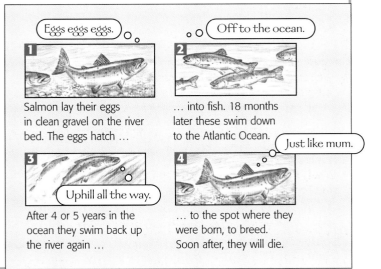

Eggs eggs eggs.

Off to the ocean.

1 Salmon lay their eggs in clean gravel on the river bed. The eggs hatch …

2 … into fish. 18 months later these swim down to the Atlantic Ocean.

Just like mum.

3 Uphill all the way. After 4 or 5 years in the ocean they swim back up the river again …

4 … to the spot where they were born, to breed. Soon after, they will die.

In this unit you'll learn how the Rhine countries are helping the river to recover, by planning, and managing, and working together.

The Rhine countries get together

By 1953 the Rhine was a smelly mess. The Rhine countries saw that the only way to clean it up was to work together. So they set up the **International Commission for the Protection of the Rhine**, or **ICPR**.

It worked slowly at first. But then in 1986 disaster struck. There was a fire in a chemical factory in Basel (Switzerland). Chemicals were washed into the Rhine by the firemen's hoses. A long stretch of the river was poisoned, affecting water supplies in all the Rhine countries. Everyone was shocked. Suddenly, cleaning up the Rhine got top priority.

The Rhine Action Programme

After the Basel fire, ICPR launched an action programme. The aim was to get the river back to health by the year 2000. By steps like these:

▲ *Dead fish in a poisoned Rhine, 1986.*

Strict limits for factory effluent all along the river. Frequent checks. Heavy fines for polluters.

Completing a scheme to build new sewage treatment works for the cities and towns along the river.

Encouraging the construction of 'fish ladders' at dams so that fish can swim upstream.

It was a success. By 2001 the oxygen in the Rhine was at a healthy level. Most pollutants had been cut by at least 70%. Some had gone completely. And the salmon were starting to return.

Not the end of the story ...

That's not the end of the Rhine story.

◆ There is still quite a lot of pollution from farming.
◆ There is still a shortage of wildlife.
◆ Storms still bring heavy flooding along the river. But in very dry summers, the water level falls so low that ships can't travel so far. (People think global warming is making these problems worse.)
◆ Many towns and cities in the drainage basin get their water by pumping up huge amounts of groundwater. So groundwater levels are falling.

▲ *Heavy flooding on the Rhine, 1998.*

... so now it's Rhine 2020

ICPR has a new action plan called **Rhine 2020**. These are its key ideas:

◆ A river and its drainage basin are a unit. So look after them both.
◆ Any action must be **sustainable**. It must balance the needs of people, and business, and wildlife. And not lead to future damage.

Rhine 2020 aims to achieve a lot by 2020. For example:

◆ get the river even cleaner, through stricter controls
◆ bring more wildlife back
◆ plant more trees in the drainage basin, to help prevent flooding
◆ return some of the river and its tributaries to their natural state (as they were before engineering works)
◆ make sure the groundwater in the drainage basin is not wasted.

In 2020, you'll be able to see how well they have done.

▲ *The fish are back in the Rhine – and so are the fishermen.*

Your turn

1

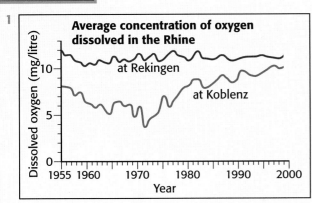

Look at this graph. Rekingen and Koblenz are two places along the Rhine.

a What causes the level of oxygen in a river to fall?
b Name one type of pollutant that can lead to a fall in oxygen.
c At which of the two places was the Rhine healthier? Explain why you think so.
d The two places are shown as **A** and **B** on the map on page 93. Which one is **A**? Explain your choice.
e In which year was the O₂ level at Koblenz lowest?
f Suggest why the level rose again, after that.
g Do you think the O₂ level will ever be the same at both places? Give your reasons.

2 In the past the Rhine countries treated their river badly. Now they are working together to manage it in a more sustainable way.

a Draw a big table with headings like this. (Full page.)

Managing the Rhine	
Old way	Sustainable way

b Now look at statements **A–P** on the right. Which do *not* show a sustainable approach? Write these in the first column of your table.

c For each statement in your first column, choose the 'opposite' one from the list, and write it in your second column.

A If we want to dam the river we'll just do it.
B We will leave the river in its natural state as far as possible.
C If my country pollutes the river, it is no-one else's business.
D We will tame the river and make it behave as we wish.
E It's okay, rivers can cope with lots of rubbish.
F If we want to dam the river we will consult the other Rhine countries first.
G We think about the whole river.
H Before we do engineering work along the river we assess its impact on the environment – and may cancel it.
I We only worry about our stretch of the river.
J We don't worry about development in the drainage basin.
K Rivers are a fragile ecosystem and we must protect them from pollution.
L Let's do the engineering work, and sort out any environmental problems later.
M Let's make sure the salmon don't die off again.
N If my country pollutes the river it affects the other Rhine countries too.
O The river is fed by its drainage basin so we must think about the drainage basin too.
P The salmon have gone. Too bad.

In this unit you'll learn about Britain's National Parks, set up to protect countryside for everyone to enjoy.

What is a National Park?

A National Park is a large area of land that is protected by law, so that it can be enjoyed by the whole nation.

So far there are 15 National Parks in Britain (the 15th set up in 2006). See the map on page 99.

How the National Parks began

100 years ago, many people worked in dirty, noisy, crowded factories, 6 days a week.

They looked forward to Sundays when they could escape to the countryside for fresh air.

But out in the countryside, landowners were busy closing off their land, and trying to keep visitors away! This made people very angry. They felt everyone had a right to enjoy the countryside. They held big meetings in the cities to protest.

At last, in 1949, the government passed a law setting up National Parks, to make sure people had access to the countryside. The first one to be set up was the Peak District National Park, in 1951.

Managing the National Parks

As you saw earlier, you need to **manage** places in order to protect them. So each National Park is managed by a **National Park Authority**. The panel on the right shows their aims.

Now use page 99 to help you answer these questions.

▲ Take to the hills!

The National Park Authority
We aim to …
◆ protect the beauty, wildlife and traditions of the Park
◆ help visitors to enjoy it
◆ promote the economic and social well-being of the people who live in it.

Hi! We're a National Park Authority.

We manage a National Park.

Your turn

1 a What is a National Park?
  b How many National Parks are there in:
    i England? ii Scotland? iii Wales?

2 Which of the UK's National Parks:
  a is largest?
  b is smallest?
  c has most residents? (Glossary?)
  d lies on the lowest land, overall? (Page 127 will help.)
  e is least crowded? (Some calculations needed!)

3 Overall, are the National Parks easy to get to? Decide, and give evidence to back up your answer.

4 The following own land in National Parks. Try to explain why they chose these areas.
  a water companies (which provide our water supply)
  b the Ministry of Defence (which runs the army)
  c the National Trust

5 a Give *five* things that *all* the UK's National Parks have in common.
  b Give *two* things that *most* of them have in common.

6 a What is a *National Park Authority*?
  b What are its aims? Write your answer in simple words that a six-year-old would understand.

7 These sheep are not keen on visitors from the city. Write a serious reply.

Keep city people out!

They don't work on the land …

… so why should they tramp all over it?

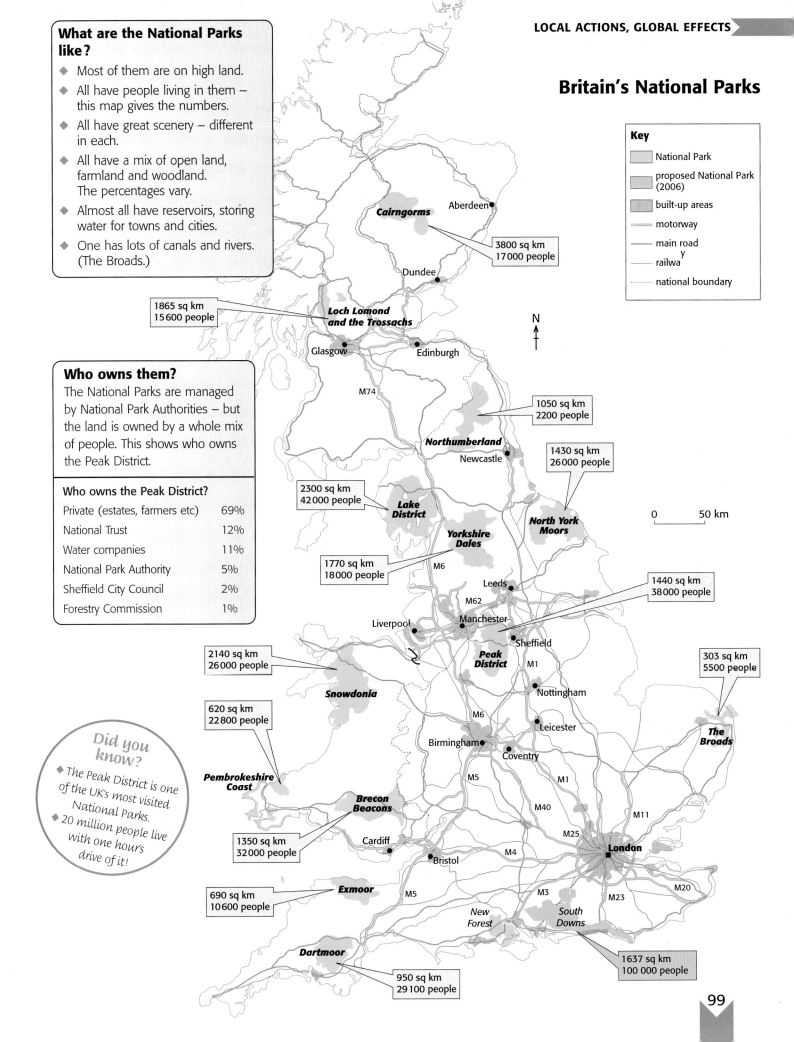

Britain's National Parks

What are the National Parks like?

- Most of them are on high land.
- All have people living in them – this map gives the numbers.
- All have great scenery – different in each.
- All have a mix of open land, farmland and woodland. The percentages vary.
- Almost all have reservoirs, storing water for towns and cities.
- One has lots of canals and rivers. (The Broads.)

Who owns them?

The National Parks are managed by National Park Authorities – but the land is owned by a whole mix of people. This shows who owns the Peak District.

Who owns the Peak District?

Private (estates, farmers etc)	69%
National Trust	12%
Water companies	11%
National Park Authority	5%
Sheffield City Council	2%
Forestry Commission	1%

Key

- National Park
- proposed National Park (2006)
- built-up areas
- motorway
- main road
- railway
- national boundary

Did you know?
- The Peak District is one of the UK's most visited National Parks.
- 20 million people live with one hour's drive of it!

Cairngorms — 3800 sq km, 17000 people

Loch Lomond and the Trossachs — 1865 sq km, 15600 people

Northumberland — 1050 sq km, 2200 people

North York Moors — 1430 sq km, 26000 people

Lake District — 2300 sq km, 42000 people

Yorkshire Dales — 1770 sq km, 18000 people

Peak District — 1440 sq km, 38000 people

The Broads — 303 sq km, 5500 people

Snowdonia — 2140 sq km, 26000 people

Pembrokeshire Coast — 620 sq km, 22800 people

Brecon Beacons — 1350 sq km, 32000 people

Exmoor — 690 sq km, 10600 people

Dartmoor — 950 sq km, 29100 people

South Downs — 1637 sq km, 100000 people

New Forest

Aberdeen, Dundee, Glasgow, Edinburgh, Newcastle, Leeds, Liverpool, Manchester, Sheffield, Nottingham, Leicester, Birmingham, Coventry, Cardiff, Bristol, London

0   50 km

M74, M6, M62, M1, M5, M40, M4, M3, M23, M20, M11, M25

In this unit you'll learn more about Britain's most visited National Park: the Peak District.

What's it like?

◆ The White Peak is a **limestone** area. It has rolling hills and deep valleys. (Look at the map.)

◆ In the Dark Peak the rock is **gritstone**. The scenery is wilder, with high moorland, bogs and steep cliffs.

◆ Between the two is an area of **shale** rock with wide fertile valleys.

◆ There are around 2500 farms in the Park. Most are small. Most rear cattle or sheep.

◆ It has 1 town and around 100 villages and hamlets.

◆ About 38 000 people live in it.

◆ It gets up to 30 million visits a year. And the visitors bring about £140 million into the area.

What can you do there?

What a choice!

☑ walking ☑ cycling ☑ climbing   ☑ pony trekking
☑ sailing   ☑ fishing   ☑ windsurfing ☑ water skiing
☑ caving   ☑ gliding   ☑ hang gliding ☑ abseiling
☑ visiting historic buildings and stately homes
☑ exploring its town, villages and hamlets

What else is it important for?

◆ **Water.** The Peak District gets plenty of rain, and has over 50 reservoirs. These supply water to towns and cities outside the park.

◆ **Quarrying and mining.** They have gone on here for thousands of years. Limestone is the main material quarried these days.

The Peak District National Park

Key

- White Peak
- Dark Peak
- road
- railway
- ● town within Park
- village ● within Park
- ● town outside Park
- ● city outside Park

0   10 km

What's quarried / mined there?

Material	Used for
limestone	road building, making cement and chemicals, and in blast furnaces
shale	making cement
gritstone	building
fluorspar	making solvents, and fluoride toothpaste!

▲ You'll find rolling hills in the Peak District …

▲ … and high wild crags too.

A closer look at its geology

Look at the rock map at the bottom of the page. If you could slice through the Peak District along the red line AB, you'd see something like this:

Key

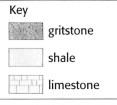

gritstone

shale

limestone

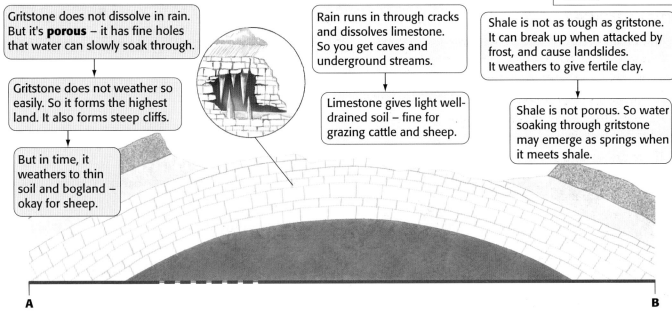

Gritstone does not dissolve in rain. But it's **porous** – it has fine holes that water can slowly soak through.

Gritstone does not weather so easily. So it forms the highest land. It also forms steep cliffs.

But in time, it weathers to thin soil and bogland – okay for sheep.

Rain runs in through cracks and dissolves limestone. So you get caves and underground streams.

Limestone gives light well-drained soil – fine for grazing cattle and sheep.

Shale is not as tough as gritstone. It can break up when attacked by frost, and cause landslides. It weathers to give fertile clay.

Shale is not porous. So water soaking through gritstone may emerge as springs when it meets shale.

A

B

Your turn

1 An American visitor asks you *where* the Peak District is. Write down your reply. It must be clear and helpful – and include at least four geographical facts.

2 See if you can explain why the Peak District:
   a gets up to 30 million visits a year
   b gets mostly day trippers
   c was the first National Park to be set up
   d has very different types of landscape.

3 These are some words to describe a place.

Objective (giving the facts)		
small	large	vast
enclosed	open	exposed
smooth	quite rough	very rough
flat	rolling	steep
grassy	wooded	thickly forested

Subjective (about feelings)		
ugly	pretty	beautiful
scary	safe	cosy
boring	interesting	inspiring
depressing	calm	exhilarating
bleak	dull	inviting

Describe the landscapes in photos **1** and **2** on page 100, and include at least two words from each set.

4 Now you have to match the two photos to **X** and **Y** on the rock map on the right.
   Write a paragraph giving reasons for your choice.

5 Geology influences scenery – and activities! In the Peak District, in which rock type would you expect to:
   a go caving?   b do some serious climbing?
   c go pony trekking?   d go sailing on a reservoir?
   e go hang gliding?   f go potholing?

6 Now, time to recap. Draw a spider map to show what you have learned about the Peak District so far. (Check Unit 7.5 too?)

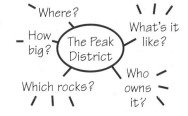

Where?
What's it like?
How big?
The Peak District
Which rocks?
Who owns it?

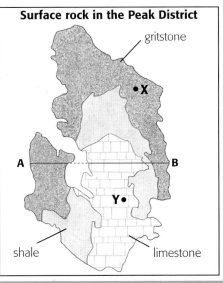

Surface rock in the Peak District

gritstone

•X

A — — — — B

Y•

shale   limestone

Here you'll read about one little village in the Peak District, that gets over 2 million visitors a year.

What's it like?

Castleton is a small neat village in the Peak District National Park. (Look for it on the map on page 100.)

We think people first settled on this site over 3000 years ago, during the Bronze Age. An ancient Iron Age hillfort overlooks it at Mam Tor. Centuries later, the Romans built a fort not far away.

But the present village dates back to around 1080, when William Peverel, an illegitimate son of William the Conqueror, built a Norman castle here.

Today, the village has only about 700 inhabitants. But they are not lonely. They get over 2 million visitors a year! Most arrive by car on Sundays in summer.

The table on the right shows the services that Castleton has to offer.

Services in Castleton

For local residents	
Service	**Comment**
Grocer	☑ 1 general store (sells a range of foods)
Butcher	☒ Nearest is 3 km away
Baker	☒ Nearest is 10 km away
Greengrocer	☒ Nearest is 3 km away
Chemist shop	☒ Nearest is 10 km away
Doctor	☒ Nearest is 3 km away
Bank	☒ Nearest is 10 km away
Post Office	☑
Church	☑ Two
Village hall	☑
Library	☒ Mobile library visits every two weeks
Petrol	☑

For visitors			
B&B / guest houses	7	Hotels	1
Camping / caravan sites	4	Youth hostels	1
Tourist shops	14	Cafés	3
Information centre	1		

For both			
Pubs (also do B & B)	6	Fish & chip shop	1

One sunny Sunday

Castleton is called a **honeypot** because it attracts swarms of visitors. There's a lot to see there, including four exciting limestone caverns. This photo was taken on the edge of the village, on a typical summer Sunday.

Did you know?
♦ Castleton is named after its Norman castle, now in ruins.

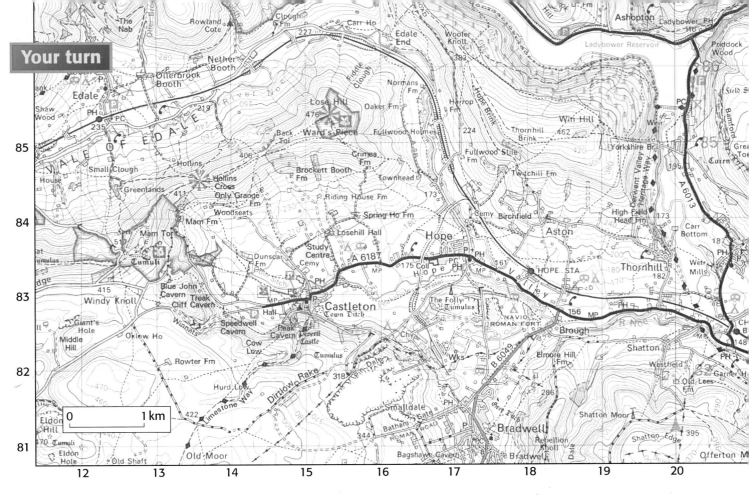

1 Look at Castleton on this OS map. Is the village on a high ridge, or in a valley? Give your evidence.

2 a Castleton is a *honeypot*. What does that mean?
  b What evidence of this can you see, in the photo on page 102?
  c Where in Castleton was the photo taken? Look for a written clue in the photo. Then try to give a six-figure grid reference on the OS map.
  d In which direction was the camera pointing?
  e What kind of rock lies below the road, in the photo? Explain how you decided.

3 Now list all the evidence you can find on the OS map, that Castleton gets lots of visitors. (Page 126 may help.)

4 Next, write a list of things visitors can see in Castleton, and underline any that *you* would find interesting.

5 Look at the services that Castleton offers (page 102).
  a How would you feel about these if you were a young mum with no car, and two small children? Explain.
  b This is what one resident thinks about Castleton. Do you agree? Give reasons.

Castleton caters better for its visitors than for its residents.

6 a First, start a table with these headings:

Living in Castleton	
Advantages	Disadvantages

  b i Now imagine you are *either*:
      A a retired person living on the main road
      B the owner and manager of a tourist shop.
      Fill in all the advantages and disadvantages you can think of, about living in Castleton, for you.
    ii Are the advantages greater than the disadvantages?
   iii Do you think your table would be different if you had chosen the other character? Explain.

7 Congestion is a problem for Castleton.
  a What does *congestion* mean?
  b Here's one person's idea for solving the problem. Do you think it's a good idea? Give reasons.

It's easy. Just build more car parks!

8 a You are in charge of managing tourism for Castleton. Come up with a bright idea for solving the congestion problem. (The OS map may help.)
  b Then write up your idea as a proposal for the local council. Add a sketch map if that helps.

Here you'll identify more of the conflicts that can arise in a National Park, and find out more about the work of the National Park Authority.

Gabriel, a farmer

Hello, I'm Gabriel. I'm a sheep farmer in the Peak District National Park, not far from Castleton. I keep a few dairy cattle too.

What's it like to live here? Well, great scenery. But sometimes I get fed up with all the visitors! They get all over my land, not just on the footpaths. They're usually clutching maps and looking lost. I get annoyed when they leave gates open. And if they let their dogs loose in my fields, with my sheep, that makes me furious.

When I go out on the tractor in summer, a ten-minute journey can take half an hour. The roads around my place are narrow, so I have to keep pulling in to let their cars past. Too bad if I'm in a hurry!

Because it's a National Park, there are lots of rules. I wanted to build a modern extension to the farmhouse, but they said 'No, it will look out of place.' Even building a wall around a field has to be done in the old way.

The Park Authority is also very fussy about what kind of business you can set up. And if you run a quarry, like my uncle, that's real trouble! All kinds of rules about noise, and trucks, and trees to hide the quarry.

Then there are all the city people who buy weekend homes here, or move here to retire. They push house prices up so locals can't afford them. My cousin Emily and her new husband had to move out of the Peak District, to get a place they could afford.

And when I go into town I feel like I'm in a theme park sometimes, with nearly every shop a tourist shop.

Still, the visitors do bring in money. And I'm hoping I'll get a share of it. When the latest plans for the extension get through, we'll do bed-and-breakfast. We'll offer big healthy organic breakfasts, with great views!

But that's enough complaining. When I get up at dawn and look out over the fields, I tell myself I'm a very lucky man.

▲ *Stepping out in the Peak District.*

▲ *Just one of those conflicts: a limestone quarry.*

◀ *Would you like to live on a Peak District farm, like this one?*

Sue, from the National Park Authority

I'm Sue. I work for the Peak District National Park Authority. I have to consult with the local council, and local people, on all kinds of issues.

It's not easy to protect an area *and* encourage visitors *and* keep the local people happy ! But that's our job ! We have to balance:

- the needs of the nation (for limestone, water and so on)
- the needs of the local people (for houses and jobs)
- the needs of the visitors (for freedom to roam, and activities, and things like car parks and toilets).

There has to be some development in the park, of course. Our job is to make sure it's sustainable. It must benefit people, but not harm the environment or lead to future damage.

▲ *The Peak District National Park Authority spreads the word.*

Your turn

1 From Gabriel's views on life in the Peak District, identify any conflicts, and say who they involve. (For example *local people can be in conflict with the National Park Authority about* ....)

2

> The National Park Authority aims to:
> ① protect the beauty, wildlife and traditions of the Park
> ② help visitors to enjoy it
> ③ promote the economic and social well-being of the people who live in it.

Below are some things the Park Authority does. For each, say which of its aims you think it's fulfilling. Give your answer like this: A = ②
(It could be fulfilling more than one !)

A It provides car parks and visitor centres.
B It helps farmers to farm in the traditional ways.
C It gives grants to repair historic buildings.
D It has rules about the materials and colours you can use for building new houses.
E It aims to limit the number of new houses, to keep the population at its present level.
F In giving permission for new houses, it gives priority to affordable homes for local people.
G It gets grants from the EU to help hill farmers.
H It forces quarry companies to plant a screen of trees around their quarries.
I It plans to improve the bus services in the Park.
J It has given planning permission to several hundred new businesses in the last 30 years.
K It looks after all the footpaths.

3 On the right are facts about the visitors to the Peak District. Look at each one. Do you think Sue and the Park Authority would like it to change ? Give reasons.

4 These pie charts compare the Peak District with the UK overall.
   a For each pair, pick out any differences you notice.
   b Then see if you can explain the differences, using what you learned in this unit.

Employment structure

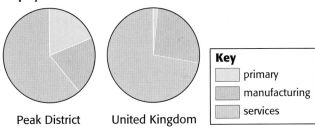

Peak District   United Kingdom

Key
- primary
- manufacturing
- services

Age structure of the population

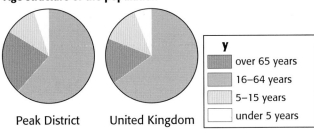

Peak District   United Kingdom

y
- over 65 years
- 16–64 years
- 5–15 years
- under 5 years

5 And finally here's one person's opinion. Do you agree? Write a serious reply.

> National Parks should be abolished now!

> **Visitors to the Peak District: some facts**
>
> A Most of them arrive by car.
> B A large number are day trippers.
> C Many bring their own picnics, from home.
> D Of those who stay over, many stay in camp sites.

Here you will learn a little about the geography of Antarctica.

The last great wilderness

Antarctica, the white continent. It is almost as big as Europe. And covered by a sheet of ice over 2 km thick on average. Try to imagine that!

Like the land under it, the ice sheet has mountains and valleys. It makes Antarctica the world's highest continent, 2300 m high on average. Its highest peak is Vinson Massif, 4897 m.

What's it like in winter?

Cold, cold, cold. The temperature falls below – 70°C in places. Take off your gloves and your fingers freeze in seconds. Get bad frostbite and they'll need to be amputated.

In winter (around June) it's dark, because Antarctica is tilted away from the sun. Thousands of km of the ocean freeze over. No ships or planes can get in. If you are stuck there in winter, without enough food or other essentials – goodbye !

What's it like in summer?

Still cold. Even the warmest parts don't get much above freezing. So you still need special clothing. But now it's bright. Some places are light all night, for a time. (The diagram on the right shows why.) Sunlight on snow can damage your eyes, so keep your goggles on.

But now planes fly in again. The ice on the ocean melts so ships can sail in. You can relax a bit. Help is at hand.

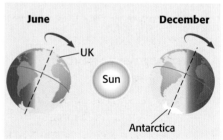

▲ Summer is when you are tilted towards the sun. So summer in the UK is winter in Antarctica, and vice versa.

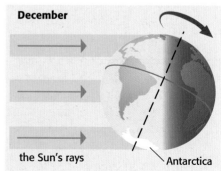

▲ In the Antarctic midsummer, some places get sunlight 24 hours a day.

A map of Antarctica

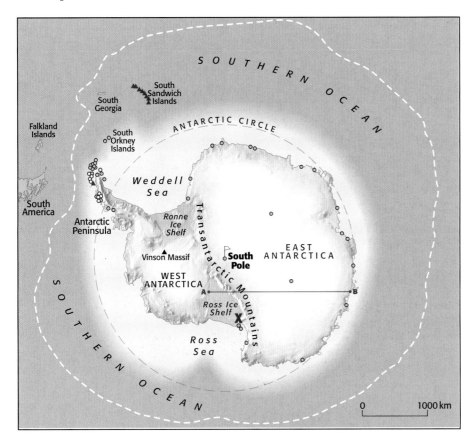

▲ *Getting to the South Pole was a great challenge for explorers. This is one of the Norwegian team who got there first – on 14 December 1911.*

Look at the Southern Ocean. It is always cold, and much of it freezes over in winter. Its boundary is called the **Antarctic Polar Front**. When you cross into another ocean, the water suddenly gets warmer.

Key
- ▨ ice shelf
- ☐ ocean iced over in winter
- ▨ rest of ocean
- ⊟ Antarctic Polar Front
- ▲ active volcano
- ▨ South American continent
- ○ main science research stations } many on
- ○ main tourist destinations } islands
- — see cross-section in 'Your turn'

Your turn

1 A small green visitor from another planet asks you where Antarctica is. Answer!

2 You're planning an expedition to the South Pole, starting from **X** on the map.
  a About how long is the journey, in a straight line?
  b Will you be able to go in a straight line? Explain.
  c In which part of the year will you travel? Why?
  d You reach the South Pole and rest overnight. What's it like there? Write an e-mail home.
  e You leave the South Pole again. In which direction are you travelling?

3 Now draw a sketch map of Antarctica. Show and label:
  West Antarctica   East Antarctica   the South Pole
  the Southern Ocean   the two seas   Ross Ice Shelf
  Ronne Ice Shelf   the Transantarctic Mountains
  Vinson Massif   the Antarctic peninsula   a volcano
  a bit of South America   the Falklands   South Georgia

4 What do you think an *ice shelf* is? (Glossary?)

5 Which oceans meet the Southern Ocean? (Page 128?)

6 At the South Pole there's daylight 24 hours a day in December and darkness 24 hours a day in June. Explain why, as if to a nine-year-old. (Use diagrams?)

7 This is a cross-section through part of Antarctica (along the red line on the map above).

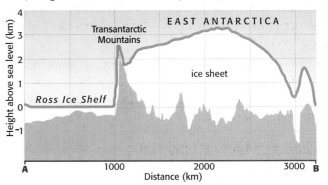

  a Is the land mostly *above* or *below* sea level?
  b About how thick is the ice at its thickest point?
  c If global warming makes the ice melt, will the UK be affected? Give reasons for your answer.

In this unit you'll learn how Antarctica was under threat from different countries – and how they now work together to protect it.

Named by the Greeks

'There is a continent at the bottom of the world,' said the Ancient Greeks, several thousand years ago. They had never seen it. But they thought it *must* exist, to balance the land at the top of the world. They named it *Anti-Arkitos* (or the opposite of *Arctic*). Soon it appeared on maps.

Captain Cook goes sailing by

Captain Cook was the first person to sail close to Antarctica, on his Second Great Voyage (1772 – 75). The British government had asked him to see if it existed. He sailed across the Antarctic Circle. He saw penguins, seals, whales and icebergs. But no continent. He sailed away again, certain that no human would ever get further south.

Then come the hunters

Captain Cook and his men sent back news of the animals they had seen. Soon ships were on their way to the Southern Ocean to hunt for seals. Some were killed for their skin, and some for their oil. By 1900 most of the seals had gone.

Whales were next. Their oil was worth a fortune. By 1965, over a *million* Antarctic whales had been killed. The whale population of the Southern Ocean was almost wiped out.

To find their prey, the sealers and whalers also had to be explorers. They mapped their routes, so the world learned more and more about the geography around Antarctica.

▲ Captain Cook: no sign of Antarctica.

Did you know?
- Britain and Norway did most of the whaling in Antarctica.
- Hull was the main British port for whaling ships.

▲ Whaling in the Southern Ocean. The whales were nearly wiped out.

▲ Curves to kill for? A strong flexible material from the whale's mouth was used in 'whalebone' corsets.

Arguing over Antarctica

While the hunters were chasing seals and whales, there were many other expeditions to Antarctica. Many were sponsored by governments, keen to find out what resources it had – and get a share!

By 1950, seven countries had laid claim to slices of Antarctica. Two others, the USA and Russia, were threatening to take it over. But in 1957, twelve countries agreed to work together there, for one year, on science projects. That was a great success. So, in 1961, they signed the Antarctic Treaty.

The Antarctic Treaty

By this treaty, countries agree to:

◆ lay aside all claims that they own Antarctica

◆ protect it as a place of peace, for scientific research

◆ ban mining and other activities that would threaten its environment.

The Antarctic Treaty has now been signed by 44 countries.

▲ *Flags around the South Pole – symbols of countries working together.*

Your turn

1 Time to draw a time line for the history of Antarctica.
   a Draw a long line, with lots of space beside it to write in. (Turn your book sideways and use two pages?)
   b Mark the line from 1770 to 1970, with a division for every 10 years.

   c Now write in the information below, at the correct places on your time line. Use small neat writing.
   d Where information covers more than one year, find a way to show this using shading.
   e And finally, give your time line a title.

> 1819–21 Russian expedition is first to see and circle Antarctica.

> 1950–58 Disputes between countries over claims to Antarctica.

> 1943 Argentina claims part of Antarctica.

> 1923 New Zealand claims part of Antarctica.

> 1839–43 British expedition led by Captain James Clark Ross explores around the Ross Ice Shelf.

> 1982 Commercial whaling is banned all over the world.

> 1800–1900 Seals hunted until almost wiped out.

> 1772–75 Captain James Cook is first to sail inside the Antarctic Circle.

> 1908 Britain claims part of Antarctica.

> 1924 France claims part of Antarctica.

> 1911 Norwegian explorer Roald Amundsen and his team are first to reach the South Pole.

> 1838–42 American expedition confirms Antarctica exists.

> 1904–1965 Whales hunted until almost wiped out.

> 1931 Norway claims part of Antarctica.

> 1933 Australia claims part of Antarctica.

> 1940 Chile claims part of Antarctica.

> 1898–1900 British expedition is first to spend a winter on Antarctica.

> 1961 Antarctic Treaty to protect Antarctica as a place of peace and science.

> 1957 Twelve countries agree to co-operate for a year on Antarctica science projects.

> 1912 British explorer Captain Robert Scott and his team reach the South Pole, 34 days after Amundsen. They perish on the return journey.

> 1897–99 Belgian expedition is first to winter inside the Antarctic Circle (trapped in ice).

Case study 3: Antarctica today

In this unit you'll learn why Antarctica is so important to us, and how the Antarctic Treaty aims to protect it.

Why is Antarctica important?

It is important for many reasons. Like these …

◆ It is the world's last great wilderness. Humans have not spoiled it.

◆ Since it has lain undisturbed for millions of years, it holds a wealth of clues about how the Earth and its atmosphere have changed over time. Scientists can search for these clues.

◆ It is a symbol of how nations can work in harmony.

Science in Antarctica

There are 16 research stations in Antarctica. About 1100 people live there right through the winter. Here are examples of the research they do:

▲ *Releasing a weather balloon in Antarctica.*

Air gets trapped in ice. So they drill out plugs of ancient ice to learn how the air has been changing. (This has helped us to understand the causes of global warming.)

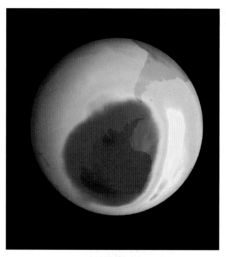

They're also learning about how pollutants get carried around in the atmosphere. Satellite images help. (This one shows the hole in the ozone layer, above Antarctica.)

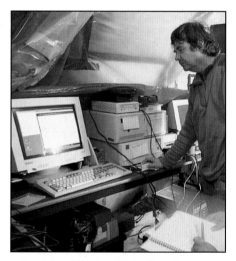

Using satellite images, they have discovered lakes hidden under the ice. Ancient species that still live in these lakes will help us understand how life evolved.

Antarctica and the ozone layer

Research in Antarctica has already helped everyone – including you!

Ozone is a form of oxygen, with the formula O_3. It collects high in the atmosphere, in the **ozone layer**. This acts as a screen, protecting us from harmful radiation from the sun.

Without ozone we'd get more skin cancers. Crops would suffer. The sea plants that fish feed on would die, so life in the ocean would collapse.

In 1985 scientists noticed that the ozone layer had a big hole in it, above Antarctica. That meant danger! (Look at the satellite image above. The blue patch is the hole. You can see Antarctica through it.)

They found the cause: solvents called **CFCs**, that were being used all over the world – for example in hair sprays, and inside fridges. When CFCs escape into the atmosphere they destroy ozone. So they are now banned.

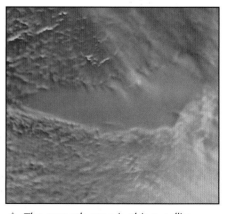

▲ *The smooth area in this satellite image shows where an ancient lake (Lake Vostok) lies under the ice.*

Threats still facing Antarctica?

The Antarctic Treaty aims to protect Antarctica from as many of the above threats as it can. For example under the treaty:

◆ rubbish must be removed from Antarctica – except waste food and sewage. (Long journeys for those would pose a health risk.)

◆ proposals for new projects must be carefully checked, to make sure they won't harm the environment. (So some get turned down.)

◆ mining for minerals is banned for the foreseeable future.

◆ fishing in the Southern Ocean is controlled.

And pressure is now growing to add strict controls for tourists.

But sadly, the Antarctic Treaty can't take care of the most serious threat of all: global warming. Look at the box on the right.

Antarctica and global warming

• Antarctica has over 90% of the Earth's ice.
• Global warming is already causing some of it to melt.
• This in turn will cause sea levels around the world to rise.
• All the world's countries need to plan, and manage, and work together FAST, to slow down global warming.
• It means we must find ways to use less fossil fuel.

Your turn

1 Look at all the reasons why Antarctica is important. Which reason do *you* think is the main one?

2 Local actions can have global effects.

a Explain how Molly's action may have affected people living in Australia.

b Now do the same for Joe.

3 Now list the threats facing Antarctica. As bullet points, in order, with the most serious one first.

4 Above are some of the Antarctic Treaty conditions to control human impact on Antarctica. Put them in what you think is their order of importance (main one first).

5 a Overall, do you think it's a good thing to have humans in Antarctica – or do you agree with this penguin?

b Write an article for *The Penguin Times*, giving your opinion, and reasons.

111

Tourism – good or bad?

The big picture

This chapter is about tourism. These are the big ideas behind the chapter:

◆ Ever since humans evolved, we have been exploring the world – and we still do, through tourism.

◆ Tourism is the world's largest industry, and it's still growing.

◆ Like any industry it will change a place, for better or worse. It can exploit people, and damage environments.

◆ Now we are learning that tourism must be sustainable.

Your goals for this chapter

By the end of this chapter you should be able to answer these questions:

◆ What are the three essential ingredients for:
a place that wants to get into tourism?
a person who wants to be a tourist?

◆ What do these terms mean?

sustainable tourism   *seasonal employment*   *package holiday*

domestic holidays   *international tourist*

◆ Why is tourism growing?

◆ Why are more people in the UK going abroad for their holidays?

◆ What else can I say about holiday patterns in the UK? (Give at least three facts.)

◆ Where is St Ives, and what attractions does it offer tourists? (Give at least four.)

◆ What are the benefits, and negative points, of tourism for St Ives?

◆ Where is Benidorm, and how has the package holiday changed it?

◆ Where is Gambia, and what does it offer tourists?

◆ What are the benefits, and negative points, of tourism for Gambia?

◆ In what ways is the Ese'eja project in Peru a good example of sustainable tourism? (Give at least five facts about it.)

And then ...

When you finish the chapter, come back to this page and see if you have met your goals!

Top 10 tourism destinations, 2002		
Rank	**Country**	**Tourist arrivals (millions)**
1	France	77.0
2	Spain	51.7
3	USA	41.9
4	Italy	39.8
5	China	36.8
6	UK	24.2
7	Canada	20.1
8	Mexico	19.7
9	Austria	18.6
10	Germany	18.0

Did you know?

◆ Tourism is the fastest growing industry on the planet.

Did you know?

◆ In 2004, 760 million people visited other countries, as tourists.
◆ In 2024, the number could be 1.5 billion.

Did you know?

◆ Around 195 million jobs around the world are connected to tourism.
◆ That's about 8% of all jobs.

Your chapter starter

The man and his camel are waiting, in the photo on page 112.

Who do you think they're waiting for?

What will happen if nobody turns up?

What country do you think this is?

Would you like a job like that?

Giddy up, camel!

Introducing tourism

In this unit you'll learn what tourists and tourism are, and what the tourist industry involves. And then uncover how much you know already !

What's a tourist?

A tourist is a person who travels to a place that's not his or her usual place, and stays there at least a night. It could be on holiday, or for business, or another purpose. But this chapter is about people on holiday.

Tourism means …

Tourism means all the activities that tourists take part in, and the services that support them. Hotels, airports, taxi drivers and ice cream sellers at the seaside are all part of the tourism industry.

It's big business …

For people on holiday, tourism means fun. For the people who look after them, it's a very serious business.

In 2002, the world's countries earned over 470 billion dollars in total, just from international tourists (from other countries). And for over 80% of all countries, tourism is one of the top five money earners. So they want to keep those tourists rolling in.

… and it's growing bigger

The tourism industry is the fastest growing industry in the world. Look at the graph on the right.

▲ *Outbound young tourists … on a school trip.*

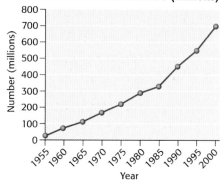

International tourist arrivals (millions)

Getting in on the act

So what does a place need, to get tourists ? These are the essentials:

1 An attraction You need an attraction of some kind to bring the tourists in. It could be a natural attraction, or built, or a mixture.

2 Accommodation and catering Tourists need places to sleep and wash. And they need food and drink. (They're only human !)

3 Transport There has to be some way for the tourists to reach the attraction – by road, or footpath, or air, or sea.

If any of these is missing, or not good enough, or spoiled, it could mean the end of your tourist industry.

For example you could ruin an attraction by allowing it to get too crowded, or polluted, or run down, so that it's no longer an attraction.

Becoming sustainable

So, as you can see, tourism needs planning and management.
And now people think it must be made sustainable. That means:

- the place, its people, and their culture, are respected
- the local people have a say in the decisions about tourism
- they gain a fair share of the benefits from it, including money
- there is as little damage to the environment as possible.

We'll come back to the idea of sustainable tourism later in the chapter.

Did you know?

- *The bad news is ... plane fuel produces carbon dioxide when it burns ...*
- *... so, more tourism means faster global warming !*

Now what about the tourists ?

There are also three essentials for being a tourist:

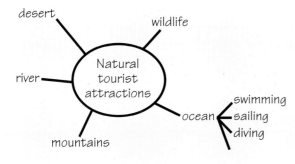

1 Time No time off would mean no holidays. Too bad !

2 Money Some people save up for their holidays all year round.

3 Inclination You must want to go somewhere. (That's the easy part.)

The growth in tourism is a sign that more and more people around the world now have all three essentials.

Your turn

1 Many countries have natural physical features, and plants and animals, that attract tourists.
   a Make a copy of the spider map started below. (Put it neatly in the middle of a new page.)

   b Add any other natural features you can think of, that might attract tourists. (Like one beginning with *v*...?)
   c Next write in all the activities tourists could take part in, based on these features.
   d Then, beside each activity, try to give an example of a place where it goes on. (In a different colour?)

2 Some tourist attractions are built, not natural. For example Disneyworld.
   a List as many others as you can.
   b After each one, write its country in brackets.

3 As well as an attraction, tourists need accommodation and catering. Copy and complete this spider map with as many examples as you can.

   hotel   B&B   Tourists need...   cafe
   accommodation   catering

4 And the final ingredient for the tourism business is … transport. Make up your own way of showing the different options for this. (Cars, coaches, and so on.)

5 Countries like tourism because it creates lots of jobs.
   a Using what you've learned on this page, list all the jobs you can think of that are connected to tourism.
   b Underline any from the primary sector in one colour, the secondary in another, and the tertiary in a third. (Add a colour key.) What do you notice?

Here you'll become a data detective, and find out for yourself about tourism in the UK, and how it's changing.

Changing patterns

250 years ago, your holiday might have been a day's outing at a fair. And only the very wealthy went abroad.

This began to change as Britain became an industrial nation. In 1871 a law was passed giving people 4 days' holiday a year – without pay. (These were the first Bank Holidays.)

Today most workers in the UK get at least 4 weeks' holiday a year, plus Bank Holidays. With pay. And tourism is very important to the economy. It earned a whopping £76 billion for the UK in 2002.

But what do people in the UK do with their holidays? And what about our overseas visitors? It's time to become a data detective.

Did you know?
◆ The UK has over 6000 tourist attractions.

Your turn

1 This question is about graph **A** on page 117.
   a What is the *overall* trend in the UK for:
      i   total holidays taken?
      ii domestic holidays (taken in the UK)?
      iii foreign holidays?
   b In which year did people first take more holidays abroad than at home?

2 Now see if you can suggest reasons why:
   a the total number of holidays increased
   b the number of foreign holidays increased
   c the *total* line is not smooth, but zig zags.
   There are clues in the box below, but you should also use what you learned in Unit 8.1. (Check back!)

CLUES

The UK economy is in better shape some years than others.

Jumbo jets can carry more people faster, further, and at less cost per person. First introduced in 1971.

Fierce competition among tour operators.

Households with use of car: 31% in 1971, 72% in 2000

UK population: 55.9 million in 1971, 60 million in 2004.

If there's a chance you'll lose your job …

TV holiday programmes

School?

Wages have been rising steadily since 1971.

Most people like sunshine.

Dishwashers, tumble driers, microwave ovens, freezers …

3 Look at map **B** on page 117. Which region of Britain was the top destination for domestic holidays? See if you can name any of its counties and attractions. (Remember, tourism needs attractions!)

4 Table **C** shows where we like to go for foreign holidays.
   a Which two countries are by far the most popular?
   b From the other named countries pick out:
      i two that seem to keep growing in popularity
      ii two that have lost appeal steadily since 1981.

5 Table **C** focuses on holidays of 4 or more nights. But are they the most popular? Table **D** has the answer!
   a Show the data from this table on a suitable graph.
   b Try to give reasons for the pattern it shows.

6 Meanwhile, lots of tourists from other countries come to the UK. Table **E** is for all kinds of tourists.
   a Which are more important to the UK economy, domestic or foreign tourists? Give your evidence.
   b On average, which group makes longer visits? Suggest reasons for this.

7 The UK was the world's 6th most visited country in 2002. Table **F** shows where the visitors came from.
   a Make a new table with these headings:

Country	Population (millions)	Visitors to UK as % of its population
Australia	19.5	3.6

   b Fill in the first two columns using the data in table F. (This has been started above.)
   c Then fill in the third column for each country, by calculating the visitors as a % of its population.
   d Draw a bar graph to show this data.
   e Explain any patterns you notice. (Language? Distance?)

8 You want to attract even more foreign tourists! Design some pages (1–3) for a website saying why the UK is a really brilliant place to visit.

A

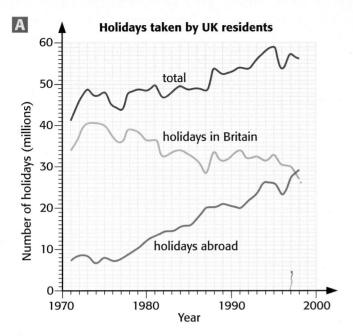

Holidays taken by UK residents

(Line graph: Number of holidays (millions) on Y-axis from 0 to 60, Year on X-axis from 1970 to 2000, showing three lines labelled "total", "holidays in Britain", and "holidays abroad")

B

Destinations for British domestic holidays, 2003

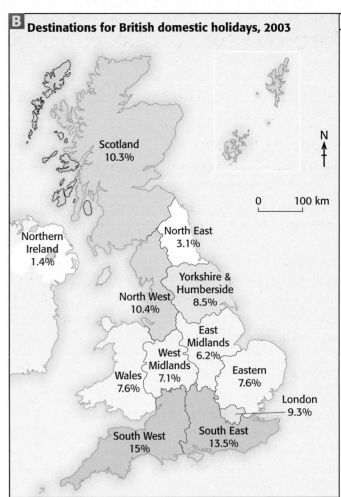

- Scotland 10.3%
- Northern Ireland 1.4%
- North East 3.1%
- North West 10.4%
- Yorkshire & Humberside 8.5%
- East Midlands 6.2%
- West Midlands 7.1%
- Wales 7.6%
- Eastern 7.6%
- London 9.3%
- South West 15%
- South East 13.5%

N

0   100 km

C

Where UK residents took their foreign holidays (4 or more nights) (%)

Country	Years 1981	1991	2001
Spain	22	21	28
France	27	26	18
Greece	7	8	8
USA	6	7	6
Irish Republic	4	3	4
Italy	6	4	4
Portugal	3	5	4
Turkey	0.1	1	2
Netherlands	2	4	3
Cyprus	1	2	4
Belgium	2	2	2
Germany	3	3	1
Malta	3	2	1
Austria	3	2	1
Other countries	10.9	10	14
Total	**100%**	**100%**	**100%**

D

Holidays taken by UK residents in 2003

Length of holiday	Number (millions)	Spending (£ billions)
1–3 nights	57.3	8.1
4–7 nights	26.2	5.9
8+ nights	7.5	2.2
Total	**91.0**	**16.2**

E

All tourism trips in the UK in 2002

	Trips (millions)	Nights (millions)	Amount spent (£ billions)
By UK residents	167.3	531.9	26.7
By overseas tourists	24.2	199.3	11.7

F

Top 10 countries of origin, for visitors to the UK in 2002 (all numbers in millions)

Country	Population	Visitors to UK
Australia	19.5	0.7
Belgium	10.3	1.0
Canada	31.9	0.7
France	60.0	3.1
Germany	82.4	2.6
Irish Republic	3.9	2.4
Italy	57.9	1.0
Netherlands	16.1	1.4
Spain	40.2	1.0
USA	287.7	3.6

▲ It's one of London's most famous attractions.

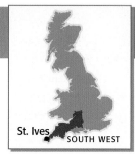

In this unit you'll explore St Ives, a popular resort for domestic holidays.

A popular resort in Cornwall

As you saw on page 117, the South West of England is popular for domestic holidays. And St Ives is one of its most popular resorts.

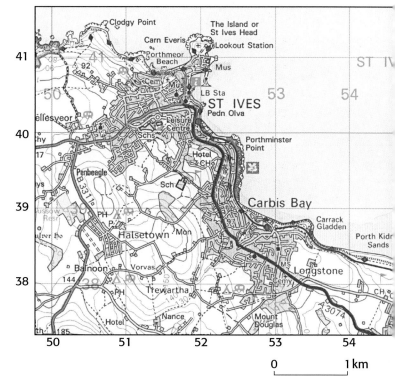

How is it doing?

St Ives is lucky. It attracts tourists because of its charm, and the unspoilt coast and countryside around it. The local council wants to keep it that way. So it aims to:

◆ improve existing accommodation for tourists (rather than build more)

◆ ensure that any new tourist developments are sustainable.

What the brochure says ...

Welcome to St Ives. Its beaches, turquoise sea, cobbled streets and secret corners will delight you.

At its heart is the fishing harbour and four great beaches. Porthmeor beach is famous for surfing. And behind the harbour lies the old part of town with its maze of narrow streets, where you can explore for hours.

At the harbour, you can watch the fishing boats unload their catches. Then treat yourself to fresh fish in one of our wonderful restaurants.

With its clear bright light, St Ives has always attracted artists. Its art galleries, studios and craft shops are sure to tempt you.

You can explore the coastline too. Ride the scenic railway from Lelant to St Ives. Take walks at your leisure, to enjoy our stunning scenery. And don't forget swimming, biking, golfing, and horseriding.

Make it a holiday to remember!

▲ St Ives: look at all those sandy beaches.

Your turn

1 Where exactly is St Ives? Answer as fully as you can.

2 Look at the building marked with a red dot on the photo. Where do you think it is on the OS map? Give a six-figure grid reference. (Hint: tower!)

3 a Draw a *large* sketch map of St Ives, showing the main physical features, the built-up area, the main road through it, and the railway.

 b Then annotate your sketch map with notes about things for tourists to do there. Use all the clues you can find on page 118.

4 Look at table **A**.

 a What can you say about the number of tourists at peak season each year, compared with the number of residents?

 b What problems might result from this? You could give your answer as a spider map.

5 Tourists visit other parts of Cornwall too. Table **B** shows data for a typical year for the whole county.

 a What do you think *number of tourist nights* means?

 b Now make a *large* copy of the diagram started below. The two vertical axes should be the same height, but different colours. (You choose.) Fill in the rest of the numbers and months.

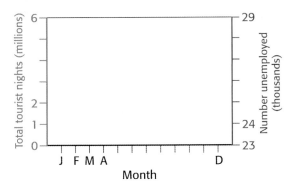

 c On your diagram:
  i plot points for the number of tourist nights, using the left axis.
  ii Join them to give a smooth line the same colour as this axis. Label the line to say what it shows.

 d Repeat for the number of unemployed residents, but this time using the right axis.

6 Look at your diagram for **5**.

 a Explain why the line graph for tourist nights is the shape it is. Try to think of more than one reason.

 b Can you see any connection between the shapes of your two graphs? Explain.

 c Much employment around St Ives is *seasonal*. What does that mean?

 d Give at least four examples of jobs in St Ives where you expect employment to be seasonal.

Use all the clues you can find on page 118.

A

St Ives / Carbis Bay		
Year	Number of residents	Number of tourists at peak season
1961	7900	8650
1971	8600	11 900
1981	9430	12 500
1991	9970	13 200
1994	9770	12 800
1996	9780	13 630

B

Cornwall through one typical year		
Month	Total number of tourist nights (millions)	Number of unemployed residents (thousands)
Jan	0.3	29.0
Feb	0.4	28.1
March	0.7	27.4
April	1.7	26.4
May	2.3	25.0
June	3.0	24.0
July	4.4	23.9
Aug	5.6	23.9
Sept	3.0	23.6
Oct	1.4	24.1
Nov	0.4	25.1
Dec	0.8	25.8

7 It's your job to bring more tourists to St Ives, especially in the quiet months. Here are three suggestions:

 A open a large hotel and conference centre for business people.

 B open a 'Harry Potter boarding school' where tourists can stay – and get lots of surprises!

 C open a 'Smugglers' Cove' telling all about the history of smuggling in Cornwall, and its famous smugglers and pirates.

 a Which do you think would be best for St Ives? Explain why you chose it and *not* the other two.

 b Prepare a short proposal for the project, to send to Cornwall County Council. Briefly describe your idea. Say which age group(s) of tourists it is likely to attract. You can even suggest a site from the map.

8 St Ives is chock full of hotels, guest houses, B&Bs, shops and eating places, that depend on tourists. But overall, is tourism good, or bad, for St Ives?

 a How could you decide? (The words *economic*, *social* and *environmental* might help.)

 b What other questions would you want to ask about St Ives, to help you decide? Try for at least five.

 c Then talk to your teacher about turning this into an enquiry!

SPAIN
Benidorm

Here you will see how tourism can change a place completely, and forever.

How Benidorm was transformed

Benidorm, in Spain, in 1960: a fishing town with 6200 residents, two great beaches and just a few hotels.

Benidorm by 1995: 55 000 residents, and 350 000 tourists at its busiest time. (Most of them British!)

And all because of the package holiday

In 1950, only 3% of people in the UK went abroad on holiday. But wages were rising. And war planes from World War II were being converted to carry passengers. So, some businessmen toured the Mediterranean looking for good holiday spots … and the **package holiday** was born.

In 1957 the first package tour, from the UK, arrived in Benidorm. The tourists loved its sunshine, peace and quiet. News spread. Soon hotels and apartments were springing up all around it to meet demand. Many had grants from the Spanish government. But there was little planning or control, and much of the building was poor quality.

> **How the package holiday works**
> - A tour operator selects a hotel.
> - It books a block of rooms for next season (or several seasons).
> - It also books some planes (or may even buy its own).
> - Then it sells a complete holiday (flight + hotel and at least some meals) to tourists.

Benidorm heads downhill

By the late 1980s, and millions of tourists later, Benidorm had a poor image.

- It was just packing people in. Look at this photo!
- It was crowded and noisy, with discos everywhere. This put many tourists off.
- Because it was cheap it attracted lots of 'lager louts'.
- Many of the hotels were shoddy and not what the brochures promised.
- There was little trace of Spanish culture, or the real Spain.

So tourists began to stay away …

Benidorm today: doing better!

Benidorm is *really* important to Spain: it contributes 1% of its GDP.
So the Spanish government got worried about its reputation.

Now the government has taken more control of its development.
Bad hotels have been improved. New posh ones have been built. A new
theme park has been set up nearby, to attract visitors all year round.

And today Benidorm gets 4 million visitors a year. (Some are day trippers.)

One problem …

There is one big problem facing the Benidorm area: water shortage!
Benidorm uses huge amounts of water for tourist swimming pools
and showers. This diagram shows what's happening:

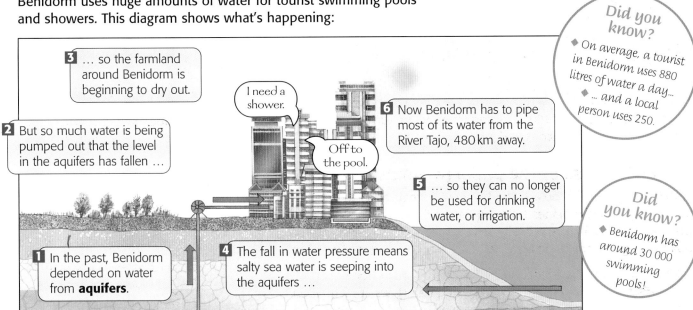

3 … so the farmland around Benidorm is beginning to dry out.

I need a shower.

6 Now Benidorm has to pipe most of its water from the River Tajo, 480 km away.

2 But so much water is being pumped out that the level in the aquifers has fallen …

Off to the pool.

5 … so they can no longer be used for drinking water, or irrigation.

1 In the past, Benidorm depended on water from **aquifers**.

4 The fall in water pressure means salty sea water is seeping into the aquifers …

Did you know?
♦ On average, a tourist in Benidorm uses 880 litres of water a day...
♦ … and a local person uses 250.

Did you know?
♦ Benidorm has around 30 000 swimming pools!

Map: ATLANTIC OCEAN, FRANCE, PORTUGAL, Madrid, River Tajo, Benidorm, IBIZA, Lisbon, SPAIN, Costa Blanca, MEDITERRANEAN SEA, AFRICA, 0 200 km

---

Your turn

1 a What were the attractions of Benidorm in 1960?
  b How has tourism affected these attractions?

2 a Make a *large* copy of the 'vicious circle' on the right.
  b Write the sentences below in your boxes, in the right order, to show how tourism can ruin a place.
  (Hint: start by writing sentence **C** in box 1.)
  A In the end, no tourists want to go there at all.
  B So developers rush to build new tourist facilities.
  C Tour operators offer cheap packages to a resort.
  D But development isn't managed or controlled …
  E Now many tourists are put off.
  F Tourists rush to book because it's so cheap.
  G … so the resort's natural attractions get ruined.
  H So the tour operators have to slash prices further.

3 Look at your vicious circle in **2**.
  a A government *could* object at step 1.
  Give a reason why it might not wish to.
  b At what point did the Spanish government intervene in Benidorm's development?
  c At what step do you think it *should* have done so?

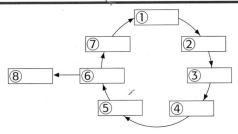

4 If tourism ruins a place, whose fault is it?
  Using your vicious circle to help you, list all the groups you think may be to blame. And give your reasons.

5 You grow almonds near Benidorm. You are worried: the soil is growing salty and your trees are dying.
  a Draw a diagram to show why this is happening.
  b Now write a letter to the Spanish government explaining why you should get compensation.

6 Do you think further growth is tourism in Benidorm is *sustainable*? Give your reasons.

7 Benidorm is beside the sea, and gets lots of sun. Come up with a sustainable way to give it as much clean water as it needs. (Hint: solar power, evaporate, condense.) Include a drawing of your scheme.

Gambling with Gambia?

Here you'll see how tourism can exploit poorer countries. We take Gambia as example.

Where is Gambia?

Gambia is a small country of 1.5 million people, in West Africa. It was created by a treaty between Britain and France in 1900. It was a British colony until 1965. It is 90% Muslim.

Today Gambia is colonised in a different way. Its climate and tropical beaches attract thousands of tourists in search of winter sun.

Gambia is keen to earn money from tourism.

The first package tour arrived (from Sweden) in 1965. Now Gambia gets around 90 000 tourists a year.

So is everyone happy?

No. Tourism has brought conflicts. Like these …

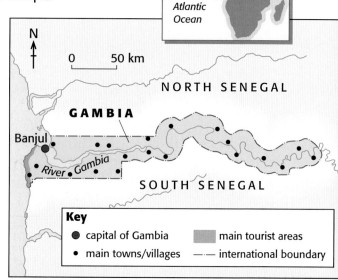

A very leaky business

Gambians are right when they say that the country does not see much of the money the tourists pay. It leaks out all over the place! Like this …

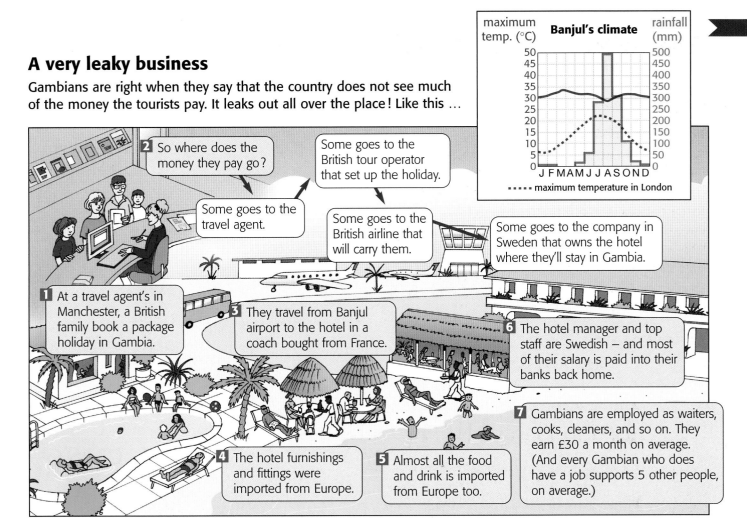

Banjul's climate

maximum temp. (°C) — rainfall (mm)

..... maximum temperature in London

2 So where does the money they pay go?

Some goes to the travel agent.

Some goes to the British tour operator that set up the holiday.

Some goes to the British airline that will carry them.

Some goes to the company in Sweden that owns the hotel where they'll stay in Gambia.

1 At a travel agent's in Manchester, a British family book a package holiday in Gambia.

3 They travel from Banjul airport to the hotel in a coach bought from France.

6 The hotel manager and top staff are Swedish – and most of their salary is paid into their banks back home.

4 The hotel furnishings and fittings were imported from Europe.

5 Almost all the food and drink is imported from Europe too.

7 Gambians are employed as waiters, cooks, cleaners, and so on. They earn £30 a month on average. (And every Gambian who does have a job supports 5 other people, on average.)

So Gambia 'owns' the natural attractions – but gets little of the tourist money. So is Gambia just being exploited?

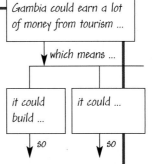

Gambia could earn a lot of money from tourism …

which means …

it could build …

it could …

so

so

Your turn

1 Using the map on page 122, write a paragraph on the geography of Gambia: where it is, physical features, roughly how long and wide it is, and so on.

2 One of Gambia's main attractions is its climate. Look at the climate graph at the top of this page.
 a Which two months are likely to bring most British tourists? Why?
 b In which three months are hotel staff most likely to be laid off? Why?

3 Look at this table comparing Gambia and the UK.

	GDP per capita (US$ PPP)	doctors per 100 000 people	% under-nourished
Gambia	1700	4	27
UK	26 200	164	very low

 a From the table, what can you conclude about:
  i the level of poverty in Gambia?
  ii the level of development in Gambia?
 b Gambians think that British tourists are wealthy. Do they have good reason for this?

4 Tourism could really help a poor country like Gambia to develop. Draw a consequence map, like the one started here, to explain why.

5 However, up to 75% of the benefits of tourism in Gambia go to other countries, not Gambia.
 a Why is that? And do you think it's fair?
 b Do you think this is *sustainable* tourism? Explain.

6 For each person below, write down what you think is:
 a the main advantage   b the main disadvantage
 of tourism:
 A the prime minister of Gambia
 B a Gambian farmer
 C a waiter in a tourist hotel in Gambia
 D a strict Muslim mum in Gambia, with four teenagers

7 You are Gambia's Minister of Tourism. You want Gambia to gain more benefit from tourism. What steps will you take? Write your answer as a speech to the Gambian parliament.

Towards sustainable tourism

Here you'll find out how sustainable tourism can benefit a poor community. We go to the rainforest in Peru for our example.

Tourism in LEDCs

Tourism is important for many LEDCs. But, like Gambia, they don't always get a fair share of the benefits from it.

They may 'own' the attractions – beautiful beaches and other scenery, a rich history, a fascinating culture, exotic wildlife.

But foreign companies (TNCs) very often own the accommodation, and provide the catering – and take away most of the profits.

The airlines that transport the tourists are usually foreign-owned too, and get paid when the holiday is booked.

So foreign companies, and foreign countries, gain most of the benefits. But the local people have to put up with the disruption that tourists bring, and the impact on their culture.

Making tourism sustainable

So, tourism can be very unfair on people in LEDCs. It is not sustainable. (Look back at the definition of sustainable tourism on page 115.)

Now pressure is growing to give people in LEDCs a say in decisions about tourism, and more chance to get involved, and a fair share of the profits. It would be fair trade, and a way to help them escape from poverty.

Example: sustainable tourism in Peru's rainforest

The Ese'eja tribe of Infierno live in a **reserve** in the Amazon rainforest in Peru. They number about 400. And they're in the tourist business !

In 1996 they signed a 20-year contract with a tour operator. They agreed to build a tourist lodge in the reserve. (They had to borrow the money.) And the tour operator agreed to bring tourists along. The deal is:

◆ the Ese'eja get 60% of the profits from the lodge
◆ they have an equal say with the tour operator, in tourism decisions
◆ they do, or are being trained to do, all the jobs in the lodge (including managing it)
◆ they act as rainforest guides for the tourists
◆ they can sell food and drink to the lodge
◆ they can sell wood carvings and other handicrafts there.

▲ *Your room awaits at the Posada Amazonas (the Ese'eja tourist lodge).*

▲ *Step up for a view of the rainforest, at the tourist lodge.*

The benefits

There are many benefits from the Ese'eja project.

◆ It brings in money for the Ese'eja people, who are very poor. They can earn by working in the lodge, or selling goods to it or through it.

◆ They are making use of their traditional skills in farming and fishing, and their knowledge of the rainforest.

◆ They are also learning many new skills (including speaking English).

◆ The rainforest has benefited too. The Ese'eja look after it very well, because it is their tourist attraction.

There are plans to show tourists more of the Ese'eja culture and way of life. But this will be done very slowly and carefully, to protect the Ese'eja.

▲ *Animals to see include capybara, like giant guinea pigs (up to 130 cm long).*

Your turn

1 The Ese'eja live in a reserve in Peru's rainforest.
   a What is a reserve?
   b Where is Peru? Which countries does it border?

2 Look back at the definition of sustainable tourism on page 115. Then think about the Ese'eja project.
   a Do you agree that it's an example of sustainable tourism?
   b Give it a mark out of 10 for sustainability, and explain why it deserves that score.

3 The tourists who stay at Posada Amazonas (the lodge) are *ecotourists*.
   a What is an ecotourist? (Glossary.)
   b Suppose you went there on holiday.
      i How do you think *you* would benefit from having Ese'ejas as hosts?
      ii How would they benefit from you?
   c Suppose lots of people hear about the place – and arrive every week in their hundreds. Do you think it could still be sustainable tourism? Explain.
   d Do you think small projects like this could solve all the problems of tourism in Gambia? Give reasons.

4 International tourism is largely run by TNCs, who like masses of tourists, on package holidays!
   A travel agent offers you a package holiday in the hotel below. Using a DCR (page 7) to help you, write down at least 8 questions to ask, to help you judge how sustainable that package operation is.

5 And finally, write an e-mail to send to the travel TNCs, saying how they could make package holidays more fair for LEDCs. Set out your advice as bullet points, in order of importance (the most important first).

Ordnance Survey symbols

ROADS AND PATHS

M I or A 6(M)	Motorway
A 35	Dual carriageway
A 31(T) or A 35	Trunk or main road
B 3074	Secondary road
	Narrow road with passing places
	Road under construction
	Road generally more than 4 m wide
	Road generally less than 4 m wide
	Other road, drive or track, fenced and unfenced
	Gradient: steeper than 1 in 5; 1 in 7 to 1 in 5
Ferry	Ferry; Ferry P – passenger only
	Path

PUBLIC RIGHTS OF WAY

(Not applicable to Scotland)

1:25 000	1:50 000	
		Footpath
		Road used as a public footpath
+++++++		Bridleway
	-+-+-+-+-	Byway open to all traffic

RAILWAYS

	Multiple track
	Single track
	Narrow gauge/Light rapid transit system
	Road over; road under; level crossing
	Cutting; tunnel; embankment
	Station, open to passengers; siding

BOUNDARIES

+ — + — +	National
+ · + · + ·	District
	County, Unitary Authority, Metropolitan District or London Borough
	National Park

HEIGHTS/ROCK FEATURES

Contour lines

· 144 Spot height to the nearest metre above sea level

outcrop cliff scree

ABBREVIATIONS

P	Post office	PC	Public convenience (rural areas)
PH	Public house	TH	Town Hall, Guildhall or equivalent
MS	Milestone	Sch	School
MP	Milepost	Coll	College
CH	Clubhouse	Mus	Museum
CG	Coastguard	Cemy	Cemetery
Fm	Farm		

ANTIQUITIES

VILLA	Roman	✕	Battlefield (with date)
Castle	Non-Roman	☆	Tumulus

LAND FEATURES

ruin	Buildings
	Public building
	Bus or coach station
} Place of Worship {	with tower / with spire, minaret or dome / without such additions
°	Chimney or tower
	Glass structure
Ⓗ	Heliport
△	Triangulation pillar
	Mast
	Wind pump / wind generator
	Windmill
+	Graticule intersection
	Cutting, embankment
	Quarry
	Spoil heap, refuse tip or dump
	Coniferous wood
	Non-coniferous wood
	Mixed wood
	Orchard
	Park or ornamental ground
	Forestry Commission access land
	National Trust – always open
	National Trust, limited access, observe local signs
	National Trust for Scotland

TOURIST INFORMATION

P	Parking
V	Visitor centre
🄸 i	Information centre
✆	Telephone
	Camp site/ Caravan site
	Golf course or links
	Viewpoint
PC	Public convenience
✕	Picnic site
	Pub/s
✝	Cathedral/Abbey
Ⓜ	Museum
	Castle/fort
	Building of historic interest
	English Heritage
	Garden
	Nature reserve
	Water activities
	Fishing
☆	Other tourist feature

WATER FEATURES

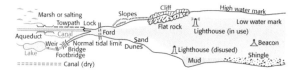

Marsh or salting Slopes Cliff High water mark
Towpath Lock Low water mark
Aqueduct Canal Ford Flat rock Lighthouse (in use)
Normal tidal limit Sand Beacon
Weir Dunes Lighthouse (disused)
Lake Bridge Footbridge Mud Shingle
Canal (dry)

Map of the British Isles

● red labels show places you study in this book

Key

- - - - - - international boundary
———— national boundary
~~~~ river
lake
▲ highest point in the UK

towns
■ largest cities
● large cities and towns

Land height
measured in metres above sea level

more than 1000 m
500 - 1000 m
200 - 500 m
100 - 200 m
less than 100 m
land below sea level

Scale 1 : 4 500 000

One centimetre on the map represents 45 kilometres on the ground.

0   45   90   135   180 km

Transverse Mercator Projection

Shetland Islands

Orkney Islands

Cape Wrath

Outer Hebrides

Lewis

Skye

NORTHWEST HIGHLANDS

Great Glen

Loch Ness

River Spey

CAIRNGORMS

River Dee

● Aberdeen

1344m ▲ Ben Nevis

GRAMPIAN MOUNTAINS

R. Tay

Mull

SCOTLAND

Dundee

Loch Lomond

Islay

Glasgow ■

River Clyde

Edinburgh ●

Firth of Forth

UNITED KINGDOM

Firth of Clyde

R. Tweed

SOUTHERN UPLANDS

CHEVIOT HILLS

NORTHERN IRELAND

North Channel

ANTRIM MOUNTAINS

R. Bann

Lough Neagh

River Erne

Belfast ●

REPUBLIC OF IRELAND

Lough Corrib

River Shannon

R. Boyne

R. Liffey

● Dublin

WICKLOW MOUNTAINS

NORTH ATLANTIC OCEAN

River Blackwater

River Suir

River Barrow

Cork ●

Isle of Man

Irish Sea

Anglesey

LAKE DISTRICT

River Eden

River Tees

PENNINES

Newcastle upon Tyne

Sunderland ●

Stockton-on-Tees ●

Middlesbrough ●

NORTH YORK MOORS

River Ouse

Blackpool ●

Preston ●

Bradford ●

Leeds ●

Kingston-upon-Hull ●

Huddersfield ●

River Aire

Bolton ● Manchester ●

River Humber

Liverpool ●

Warrington ●

Stockport ●

River Mersey

Sheffield ●

Castleton ●

PEAK DISTRICT NATIONAL PARK

ENGLAND

Stoke-on-Trent ●

Ollerton ●

R. Dee

Derby ●

Nottingham ●

The Wash

R. Wensum

Telford ●

R. Trent

Leicester ●

THE FENS

Norwich ●

CAMBRIAN MOUNTAINS

Walsall ●

Wolverhampton ●

Birmingham ■

Coventry ●

Peterborough ●

Cardigan Bay

Dudley ● Solihull ●

Northampton ●

R. Great Ouse

Ipswich ●

WALES

R. Severn

River Avon

Milton Keynes ●

R. Stour

River Teifi

R. Wye

COTSWOLD HILLS

CHILTERN HILLS

Luton ●

River Tywi

River Usk

Basildon ●

BRECON BEACONS

Newport ●

R. Thames

London ■

Southend-on-Sea ●

Swansea ●

Cardiff ●

Reading ●

St George's Channel

Bristol ●

SALISBURY PLAIN

NORTH DOWNS

Bristol Channel

EXMOOR

SOUTH DOWNS

Strait of Dover

NORTH ATLANTIC OCEAN

R.Exe

Southampton ●

Bournemouth ●

Poole ●

Portsmouth ●

Brighton ●

Isle of Wight

DARTMOOR

St Ives

Land's End

Isles of Scilly

Torbay ●

Plymouth ●

English Channel

North Sea

127

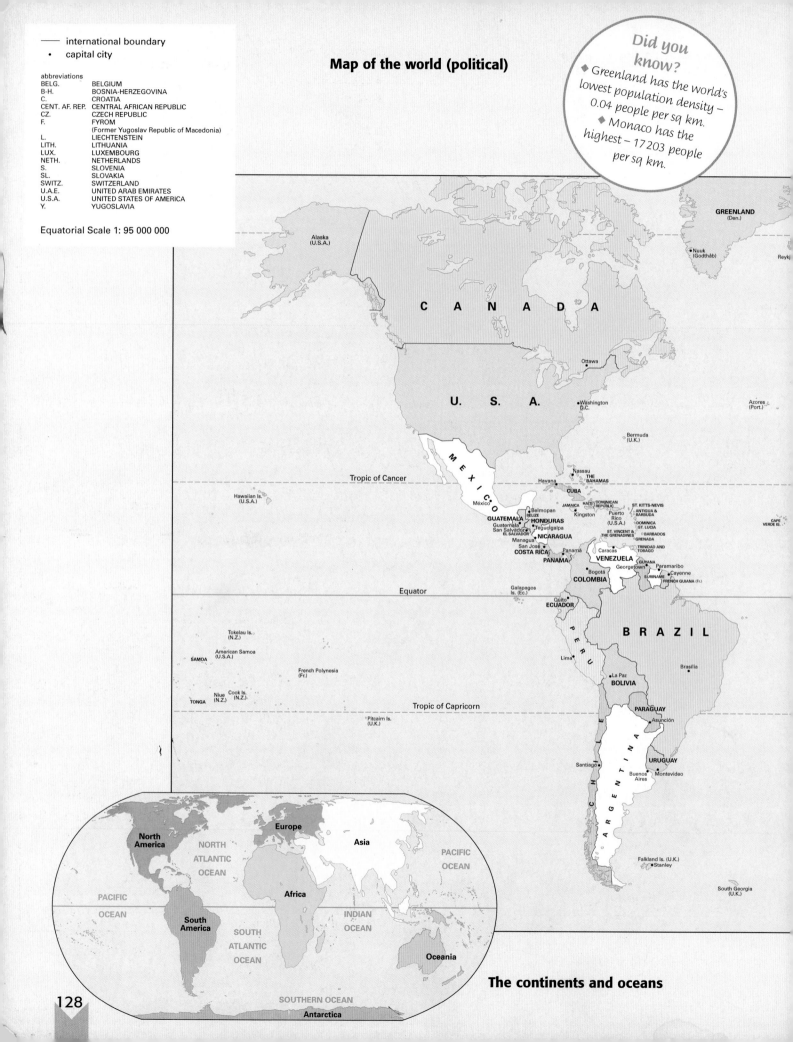

Map of the world (political)

Did you know?
◆ Greenland has the world's lowest population density – 0.04 people per sq km.
◆ Monaco has the highest – 17 203 people per sq km.

GREENLAND
(Den.)

Alaska
(U.S.A.)

• Nuuk
(Godthåb)

Reykj

C A N A D A

Ottawa

U. S. A.

• Washington
D.C.

Azores
(Port.)

Bermuda
(U.K.)

Tropic of Cancer

Hawaiian Is.
(U.S.A.)

Nassau
• THE
BAHAMAS

Havana
CUBA

M
E
X
I
C
O

México •

DOMINICAN
REPUBLIC

JAMAICA HAITI

ST. KITTS-NEVIS
ANTIGUA &
BARBUDA

CAPE
VERDE IS.

Belmopan
BELIZE

Puerto
Rico
(U.S.A.)

DOMINICA
ST. LUCIA

GUATEMALA

Kingston

HONDURAS

Guatemala •
San Salvador •
EL SALVADOR

Tegucigalpa

ST. VINCENT &
THE GRENADINES

BARBADOS
GRENADA

NICARAGUA

Managua •
San José •
COSTA RICA

TRINIDAD AND
TOBAGO

Panamá •
PANAMA

Caracas •

VENEZUELA

GUYANA

Paramaribo
•

Equator

Bogotá •

Georgetown
SURINAME

Cayenne
FRENCH GUIANA (Fr.)

COLOMBIA

Galapagos
Is. (Ec.)

Quito •
ECUADOR

B R A Z I L

P
E
R
U

Tokelau Is.
(N.Z.)

American Samoa
(U.S.A.)

SAMOA

French Polynesia
(Fr.)

Lima •

Brasília •

La Paz •

BOLIVIA

Niue Cook Is.
(N.Z.) (N.Z.)

TONGA

Tropic of Capricorn

PARAGUAY

Asunción •

Pitcairn Is.
(U.K.)

C
H
I
L
E

A
R
G
E
N
T
I
N
A

URUGUAY

Santiago •

Buenos
Aires

Montevideo

Falkland Is. (U.K.)
• Stanley

South Georgia
(U.K.)

The continents and oceans

North
America

NORTH
ATLANTIC
OCEAN

Europe

Asia

PACIFIC
OCEAN

PACIFIC

OCEAN

Africa

INDIAN
OCEAN

South
America

SOUTH
ATLANTIC
OCEAN

Oceania

SOUTHERN OCEAN

Antarctica

Population of the world's continents

- ◆ Asia — 3.92 billion
- ◆ Africa — 0.90 billion
- ◆ Europe — 0.72 billion
- ◆ N America — 0.48 billion
- ◆ S America — 0.35 billion
- ◆ Oceania — 0.03 billion

The world's top five languages (native speakers)

- ◆ Chinese (Mandarin) — over 1 billion
- ◆ Hindi — 498 million
- ◆ Spanish — 391 million
- ◆ English — 512 million
- ◆ Arabic — 245 million

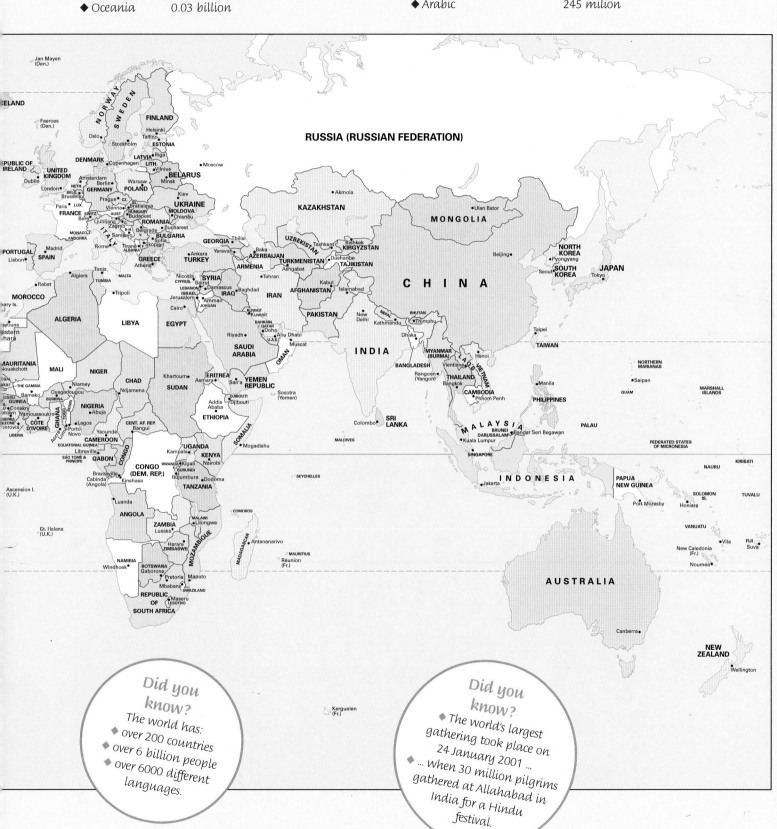

Did you know?
The world has:
- ◆ over 200 countries
- ◆ over 6 billion people
- ◆ over 6000 different languages.

Did you know?
- ◆ The world's largest gathering took place on 24 January 2001 …
- ◆ … when 30 million pilgrims gathered at Allahabad in India for a Hindu festival.

Glossary

A

acid rain – rain with acidic gases dissolved in it; it can kill fish and plants

adult literacy rate – the % of people aged 15 and over who can read and write a simple sentence

agricultural economy – term used for a country that depends mainly on farming

aid – help given by richer countries to poorer countries

annotate – add notes (not just labels) to a map, diagram, text or photo

Antarctic Treaty – the treaty that aims to protect Antarctica as a place of peace and scientific research

aquifer – an area of rock below the ground, that holds water like a sponge

B

bacteria – tiny organisms, each just one cell; some are harmless, some cause disease

bauxite – aluminium ore

bilharzia – a disease caused by tiny worms found in river water; you get fever and may suffer kidney and brain damage

biodegradeable – bacteria can break it down

brand name – a name that shoppers recognize (like McDonald's)

brownfield site – a site that was already built on, and is being redeveloped

C

call centre – where people are employed to work all day long on the phone (for example in telephone banking)

cholera – a disease caused by bacteria in dirty drinking water (diarrhoea, vomiting, and you can die from dehydration)

climate – the 'average' weather in a place

colliery – a coal mine and its buildings

colonised – taken over and ruled by another country

colony – a country taken over and ruled by another country

commodity exchange – a trading centre where commodities like coffee, cocoa, and sugar are bought and sold on the world market

congestion – overcrowding; traffic jams

conurbation – a continuous built-up area where towns and cities have joined

D

debt – what you owe to someone

decentralise – to spread out an industry so that it's not all concentrated in one area

decline – draw to an end

deforestation – when forests are cut down

delta – flat area of deposited material at the mouth of a river, where it enters the sea

demand – the total amount of a good or service that people are willing to buy

desertification – when soil in a savanna region gets dried out, and useless

development – a process of change for the better in a place; the changes improve people's lives

development compass rose – a framework based on the compass to help you ask questions about people and their lives

development indicators – data used to compare how developed countries are

domestic holiday – taking a holiday in the country you live in

drainage basin – the land around a river, from which water drains into the river

E

economic – to do with the economy, money and earning a living

economic activity – work you get paid for

economic indicators of development – indicators such as GDP per capita that tell you how wealthy a country is

ecosystem – a unit made up of living things and their non-living environment (soil, warmth, water, and so on)

ecotourism – where tourists focus on the plants and animals in an ecosystem

effluent – waste liquid (from factories)

electronic goods – goods such as mobile phones and computers that depend on a computer chip

employment structure – tells you what % of the workforce is in each employment sector (primary, secondary, tertiary)

environmental – to do with the environment (air, soil, water, wildlife and so on)

EU (European Union) – the 'club' of European countries that co-operate with each other about trade and other issues

exploit – to make use of someone, in an unfair way, for profit

F

fair trade – where the producer of the goods gets a fair share of the profits

Fairtrade Foundation – the organisation that gives companies the right to use the Fairtrade logo, and checks up on them

free trade – when countries trade freely with each other, with no restrictions

fertilisers – substances put on soil to help crops grow

fledgling industry – a new young industry that is not very strong yet

G

GDP – (gross domestic product) – the total value of all the goods and services produced in a country in a year

GDP per capita – the GDP divided by the population: it gives you an idea of how wealthy the people are, on average

globalisation – the way companies, ideas and lifestyles are spreading round the world with increasing ease

global warming – temperatures around the world are rising; scientists have linked this to the carbon dioxide produced when we burn fossil fuels

GNI (gross national income) – the total amount earned in a year in a country (including money coming in from other countries), minus what it has to pay out to other countries

H

HDI (human development index) – a 'score' between 0 and 1 to indicate how developed a country is; the higher the number, the better

heavily indebted countries – poor countries with large loans they can't repay

heavy industry – traditional 'bulky' industries such as coal mining, steel making, and ship building

hemisphere – half of the globe; the northern hemisphere is the half that's north of the equator

Le Hexagon – France gets called this (because it is shaped like a hexagon)

High Street banks – banks with branches in many towns and cities (eg NatWest)

honeypot – a place that attracts swarms of tourists and day trippers

hydroelectricity – electricity generated when running water spins a turbine

I

ice shelf – a very thick floating ice sheet attached to the coast

IMF (International Monetary Fund) – a fund set up by governments to make loans to countries, especially for trade

in decline – coming to an end, dying away

Industrial Revolution – the period of history (around the 18th century) when many new machines were invented and many factories built

infant mortality – the number of babies out of every 1000 born alive, who die before their first birthday

interdependence – how countries depend on each other, eg for trade and tourism

interest (on a loan) – the charge for taking out a loan; it is a % of the loan

international tourist – a tourist from another country

irrigation – bringing water to water crops

L

leakage – how the money tourists pay 'leaks away' from the destination country

LEDC – less economically developed country (one of the poorer countries)

life expectancy – how many years a new baby can expect to live, on average

local actions, global effects – how actions we take can affect people and places in other countries (for better or worse)

M

machete – a broad heavy knife used for harvesting crops, and other tasks

MEDC – more economically developed country (one of the richer countries)

media – different forms of communication, including radio, TV and newspapers

metropolitan area – a city plus the surrounding area that is very closely linked to it, socially and economically

migrate – to move from one area or country to another (perhaps for work)

Millennium Development Goals – goals, agreed by world leaders, to reduce poverty in the world by the year 2015

millet – a type of cereal crop

N

National Park – a large area protected by law for the benefit of everybody

National Park Authority – the body that manages a National Park

natural increase – the birth rate minus the death rate, for a place

natural resources – resources that occur naturally, such as oil wells, fertile soil

net migration – the number of people moving into an area minus the number moving out

NGO (non-governmental organisation) – an organisation such as Oxfam, that is independent of the government

O

ozone layer – the layer of ozone gas high in the atmosphere which protects us from the sun's most harmful radiation

P

package holiday – where you pay in advance for travel and accommodation

pesticides – chemicals sprayed on crops, to kill insects that might eat them

pollution – anything that spoils the environment, such as soot or harmful fumes from factory chimneys

poor south – a term sometimes used for poorer countries (since many are in the southern hemisphere)

population density – the average number of people per square kilometre

population distribution – how the population is spread around the country

porous – has tiny holes that let water through; gritstone is a porous rock

PPP (purchasing power parity) – means a figure (such as GDP) has been adjusted to take into account that a dollar buys more in some countries than others

primary sector (of the economy) – where people are employed in collecting things from the earth (farming, fishing, mining)

processing – converting a material from one form to another (for example cotton to denim, or milk to cheese)

profit – left when you subtract the cost of something from what you sold it for

PV cell – cell that converts sunlight straight into electricity; it provides solar power

Q

quaternary sector (of the economy) – involved in hi-tech research

R

raw material – material that has not yet been processed; for example cotton before it is woven into cloth

redevelop – to change or improve a site that has already been in use

relief – the shape of the land (how high or low it is)

reserve – an area set aside for a purpose, for example as a place where a rainforest tribe can live in peace

residents – the people who live in a place

revenue – money you take in from selling goods and services

rich north – a term sometimes used for the richer countries (since most are in the northern hemisphere)

rural – to do with the countryside

rural depopulation – when the population of a rural area falls (usually because people move away to find work)

S

secondary sector (of the economy) – where people work in manufacturing

service sector – see *tertiary sector*

slave trade – the buying and selling of people to work as slaves (without pay)

social – to do with the way people live

socio-economic – to do with how people live and earn their living (from *social* and *economic*)

solar power – uses energy obtained directly from sunlight; see *PV cell*

subsidies – grants (eg for growing a crop)

supply – the total amount of a good or service that is available to buy

sustainable – can be continued into the future without harm

sustainable development – development that contributes to social, economic and environmental well-being

sustainable tourism – where the local people have a say, and gain economic and social benefits, and the environment is not harmed

sweatshop – a place where people are forced to work long hours for low pay

T

tariff – a tax that a country places on goods being imported or exported

tertiary sector (of the economy) – where people are employed in providing services (like medical care and transport)

Third World – a name sometimes used for the world's poorer countries

Third World debt – the money owed by the poorer countries to the richer ones

TNC (transnational corporation) – company with branches in many countries

tourism – everything to do with tourists, including the activities they take part in and the services that support them

tourist – a person who stays for more than a day in a place that is not his or her usual environment, for any purpose

toxic – poisonous

typhoid – a disease you can get from dirty drinking water; you suffer fever and pains in your abdomen, and may die

U

under-five mortality rate – the % of babies born alive who die before they reach five

undernourished – when you don't get enough food to live a normal healthy life

unemployment – when people want to work but can't find a job

W

water table – the upper surface of the groundwater held in rocks

World Bank – a joint bank owned by governments of over 180 countries, set up to provide loans for development

WTO (World Trade Organisation) – a body set up to help trade between countries; over 140 countries belong to it

Index